EROTIC TALES OF
MEDIEVAL GERMANY

MEDIEVAL AND RENAISSANCE TEXTS AND STUDIES

VOLUME 328

MRTS TEXTS FOR TEACHING
VOLUME 3

Erotic Tales of Medieval Germany

Selected and Translated
by
Albrecht Classen

with a contribution by Maurice Sprague

And with an edition of Froben Christoph von Zimmern's
"Der enttäuschte Liebhaber"

ACMRS
(Arizona Center for Medieval and Renaissance Studies)
Tempe, Arizona
2007

Library of Congress Cataloging-in-Publication Data

Erotic tales of medieval Germany / selected and translated by Albrecht Classen;
with a contribution by Maurice Sprague ; and with an edition of Froben
Christoph von Zimmern's "Der enttäuschte Liebhaber".
    p. cm. -- (Medieval and renaissance texts and studies ; v. 328)
    Includes bibliographical references.
    ISBN-13: 978-0-86698-374-7 (alk. paper)
  1. German poetry--Middle High German, 1050-1500--Translations into English.
2. Erotic poetry. 3. Narrative poetry, German. 4. Tales, Medieval. I. Classen,
Albrecht. II. Sprague, Maurice. III. Zimmern, Froben Christof, Graf von, 1519-
1566 or 7. Enttäuschte Liebhaber. English.
    PT1417.3.E5E7 2007
    831.008--dc22

                                                                2007009709

∞
This book is made to last.
It is set in Adobe Kepler Std,
smyth-sewn and printed on acid-free paper
to library specifications.
Printed in the United States of America

TABLE OF CONTENTS

Introduction to the Genre: The mære

Names such as Giovanni Boccaccio, Geoffrey Chaucer, Franco Sacchetti, and perhaps also Poggio Bracciolini and Marguerite de Navarra easily come to mind when we think of medieval short verse narratives, or erotic, often also didactic and moral tales. Wolfgang Spiewok[1] claimed, however, that there was also a German *Decameron*, except that this would have to be compiled from numerous miscellany manuscript collections containing a vast corpus of Middle High German verse narratives generally known as *mæren*. These *mæren* are, similar to their European parallels, fairly short verse narratives of erotic, moral, didactic, sometimes also social and political content, consisting of ca. 150 to ca. 2000 verses. They were mostly composed between ca. 1250 and 1500 and exerted a considerable influence on public opinion. Some of these *mæren*, of which about two hundred to two hundred and twenty are known to us, have been preserved only in one or two manuscripts, while others have come down to us in ten to twenty manuscripts. Collectors were obviously greatly interested in this literary genre, as indicated by some of the great miscellany manuscripts, such as Heidelberg Cpg 341, Vienna 2885, Dresden M 68, Vienna 2705, Munich Cgm 270, Karlsruhe 408, and so forth. But a clear definition of *mæren* proves to be difficult, and many times these collections contain numerous texts that belong to other genres as well.

Originally, the term *mære* in classical Middle High German denoted a range of meanings, such as 'news,' 'account,' 'a novelty,' 'report,' 'a literary source,' 'book,' and 'narrative,' and was fully integrated into the common language of courtly romance and heroic epic. Only in the thirteenth century did the term *mære* emerge as a formulation characterizing a specific literary genre as defined above. Fables, on the other hand, are not *mæren*, despite various formal similarities, whereas the latter genre proves to be closely related to the Old-French *fabliau* and the Latin *ridicula*. In a number of cases it might be difficult to distinguish clearly enough between a *mære* and related genres, such as *bîspel* or *Minnerede*, both focusing on didactic and erotic aspects respectively in a rather abstract fashion. But overall, *mæren* are best described as entertaining narratives that deal with marital problems, gender conflicts, and issues concerning everyday-life situations, mostly in an urban set-

---

[1] *Altdeutsches Decamerone*, ed. and trans. Wolfgang Spiewok, 2nd ed. (1982; Berlin: Ruetten & Loening, 1984).

ting, but sometimes also within the village community, as we can observe in the case of the earliest *mæren* by The Stricker. The authors do not pay much attention to religious issues and display very little respect for the church, often depicting adulterous priests and monks, duped clerics, and foolish confessors.

The sexual component figures prominently in many *mæren*, and yet the poets clearly shy away from possible pornographic features. Once we come to the fifteenth century, however, this proviso no longer applies, at a time when graphic elements and grotesque forms of violence become noticeable.

In fact, one of the most important functions of *mæren* seems to be to provide literary entertainment that is often predicated on the erotic, but fundamentally oriented toward pragmatic advice about proper behavior within the city community. Despite many misogynistic statements, often the female figures put their male partners to shame because of their superior morality, or because of their independent minds that allow them to pursue their own path toward individual happiness. Stupid and silly behavior proves to be a favorite butt of the joke, since the intelligent protagonist enjoys the highest respect and triumphs over all hindrances. All this indicates the strong similarities or close thematic ties between Middle High German *mæren* on the one hand, and Old French *fabliaux* and Italian/Latin *fazetiae* on the other. In fact, the web of intertextual connections between these German narratives and the international short narrative literature, extending far into the high Middle Ages (in Latin), and including Jewish (Hebrew) and Arabic literatures, always needs to be kept in mind.

Some of the *mæren* authors belonged to the class of lower nobility (Herrand von Wildonie, Wilhelm Werner von Zimmern, and Egenolf von Staufenberg). Others can be identified as court administrators, such as Dietrich von der Glezze and Heinz der Kellner, but the largest number usually were representatives of the urban intelligentsia: administrators, scribes, craftsmen as dilettante writers, and others.

Many *mæren* have come down to us anonymously, but we know by name at least some of the most significant authors, such as The Stricker, Konrad von Würzburg, Heinrich Kaufringer, Hans Folz, Hans Rosenplüt, Herrand von Wildonie, Johannes von Freiberg, Jacob Appet, Ruprecht von Würzburg, and Rüdeger der Hinkhofer. Sometimes, however, a poet's self-identification does not necessarily correspond to reality, as we can see in the case of one tale by 'Konrad von Würzburg'. Here the name seems to have been used by another poet to profit from Konrad's considerable authority and thereby to secure success for his own tale.

The genre itself experienced an amazing longevity, beginning sometime in the early thirteenth century, when it was basically invented by an Austrian goliardic poet known only as The Stricker (The Weaver), and continuing at least until the first half of the sixteenth century. The famous *Ambraser Heldenbuch*, for instance, which Hans Ried wrote between 1504 and 1516 on behalf of Emperor Maximilian I, contained a number of significant *mæren* originally composed as early as the thirteenth century. And the famous Nuremberg shoemaker and poet Hans Sachs (1494-1576) continued to write *mæren* as well, though the genre disappeared altogether by the end of the sixteenth century.

Mæren were created in many areas of the German-speaking lands, such as Upper and Lower Austria, Styria, Tyrol, Bavaria, Swabia, Alsace, Franconia, Hessia, Thuringia, Saxony, and Bohemia, but not so often west of the Rhine or north of the Main. The targeted audience seems to have been fairly well informed about the canon of Middle High German literature, as repeated references to such texts as Wolfram von Eschenbach's *Parzival*, Gottfried von Strasbourg's *Tristan*, Hartmann von Aue's *Erec*, the anonymous *Nibelungenlied*, and then the *Rabenschlacht*, among others, indicate.

The authors were obviously concerned with the well-being of their society and harshly criticized shortcomings on an individual and a public level. The erotic aspect dominates, especially the question of how a happy marriage can be maintained.[2] But evil and stupid marriage partners do not fare well, and violence easily erupts. Many *mæren* reflect upon the world of the urban class, but life within a courtly setting also plays a significant role. Through many comic elements the authors of these *mæren* attempted to criticize social, moral, ethical, but also economic, political, and religious shortcomings.

These *mæren* prove to be small masterpieces of medieval German literature, and many would easily stand the comparison with tales included in Boccaccio's *Decameron* or Chaucer's *Canterbury Tales*. Especially Heinrich Kaufringer and Dietrich von der Gletze (Glesse) deserve our recognition for their delightful, multilayered, provocative, and highly complex narratives.

The following selection and translation can only hope to whet the reader's appetite and bring into relief a vast corpus of most intriguing, fascinating, and entertaining German verse narratives from the late Middle Ages. But I also believe that the selection contains some of the best examples of Middle High German *mæren* that deserve to be studied in greater detail, both by themselves and in comparison with the European narrative tradition.[3]

I created these translations primarily with my students in mind, and since I worked on many of these translations during my 2006 Summer Medieval Travel

---

[2] A. Classen, *Der Liebes- und Ehediskurs vom hohen Mittelalter bis zum frühen 17. Jahrhundert* (Münster: Waxmann, 2005).

[3] Cf. Robert J. Clements and Joseph Gibaldi, *Anatomy of the Novella: The European Tale Collection from Boccaccio and Chaucer to Cervantes* (New York: New York University Press, 1977).

Course in Europe, I would like to dedicate this little book to my travel companions, a group of wonderful young people:

Stephen Arougheti, Jessica Baker, Katherine Bruhn, Jeff Crawford, Bonnie Florez, Erin Frame, Eric Fuhrmann, Grant Gephart, Brianne Gonzales, Kelly Griffin, Shannon Hubbard, Benjamin Katzenberg, Rebecca Kelly, Jocelyn Kuhn, Ingrid Lindstrohm, Aimee Marques, Rebecca Noreen, Sara Shook, Melissa Taylor, and Sarah Woods.

I hope you will enjoy these texts!

About This Translation

Rendering late medieval German verse narratives into English represents a considerable challenge and requires a number of preliminary decisions as to the procedure in handling such a task and the necessary compromises to achieve this goal. Many questions need to be answered at first: should the verse structure be replicated, or would it be better to translate the original verse into modern prose? Should the English text stay very close to the original, even when syntactical or lexicographic problems occur there? How closely should metaphorical and idiomatic phrases be translated, if at all possible, into English? If we stick to a verse-to-verse translation, should we also try to imitate the rhyme scheme and the meter? What do we do in a case of *anacoluthon* (an irregular arrangement of sentence particles)? Or *hysteron proteron* (the later event comes before the earlier)? Or *anadiplosis* (repetition of a word or a sentence in subsequent lines)? Or *pleonasm* (a redundant phrase)? These and other features might be the results of deliberate rhetorical strategies, or they could be, as I would tend to believe in the case of our verse narratives, rather simple shortcomings on the part of the poets, or features necessary for the musical performance, since practically all medieval secular narratives were accompanied with music.

Looking at the task at hand, there are a number of reasons why these verse narratives prove to be difficult to translate, whether on the level of the grammar or the lexicon, or regarding the meaning of individual expressions. Many words cannot be found in the standard medieval dictionaries (e.g., Lexer, *Mittelhochdeutsches Handwörterbuch*); dialect variations become noticeable and might be untranslatable altogether; and idiosyncratic features by the various poets at times would require flexible approaches. Repeatedly the authors utilized simply for the sake of the rhyme or the meter phrases that should be dropped altogether in the English translation, or they employed anaphoras in the rendering of dialogues (He said/She said), and here it seemed most pragmatic and adequate to add names or nouns to clarify who is speaking at specific moments. Countless times it was necessary to translate the verses by first rearranging them in the original in order to establish a logical English sentence. This was particularly helpful since there was no need, according to my choice of translating the original texts into prose, to pay attention to the rhyme scheme.

Every translator faces these and other difficulties, and each effort to do justice to the original requires new efforts, new compromises, and new solutions. No translation is like any other, and each translation represents a negotiation with the source, either staying very close to it or taking the liberty to express things in a kind of paraphrase, or by relying on the specific words in the target language.

There are very good reasons to translate the Middle High German verses into English by resorting to simple prose, but I include the verse numbers for every block of five verses, making it possible easily to check the source against the translation. My goal was not to imitate the source in verse and to offer an aesthetically, or poetically, matching English prose text; instead I wanted to make the original available in straightforward English prose to help the reader understand the narratives as concretely and specifically as possible. The necessary compromise involved, and this at times (regrettably though unavoidably for philological reasons) at the cost of the flow of the language, a certain awkwardness in the use of images and metaphors, and at the cost of occasional repetitions. I hope, however, still to have provided a good reading of these *mæren* and to have made available a short selection that will satisfy the philologist and the general reader alike. The compromises that I accepted might occasionally be too much for one or the other side, but the verse references make it very easy to check the original against my translation.

At the top of each individual selection I provide a short blurb with literary and historical background information, followed by a reference to the work I drew the original from. I have also each time specified the date of composition, as far as we can tell today, and identified the manuscript situation relevant for each text. Contrary to possible expectations by strict philologists, I have opted to leave out the original Middle High German text, not reproducing it on the facing pages because it would not serve the intended purpose of this little book. The reader can always find the original easily through the reference given after each introduction, whereas the inclusion of the original would have doubled the size and price of this book.

As far as I can tell, these texts have never been translated into English before, and I hope that this selection and translation will open new avenues of comparative research for scholars dedicated to the late Middle Ages. I also hope that the reading public will accept this short anthology as an invitation to explore further the many jewels in late medieval German *mæren* that offer surprisingly much erotic and religious, moral and didactic entertainment, social and political criticism, and important insights into complex gender relations. Wolfgang Spiewok might have been too enthusiastic in choosing the title *Altdeutsches Decamerone* (Old German *Decameron*) for his German translation of a much larger selection, especially since he combined numerous verse narratives from different authors and different manuscripts, whereas Boccaccio created his *Decameron* (ca. 1350) all by himself. And Spiewok offered a translation that often proves to be very loose and tends to paraphrase instead of closely rendering the original into the modern language (German), more often than not simply ignoring difficult passages. But I would agree with him that the vast corpus of Middle High German verse narratives shares many of the features that highlight Boccaccio's and comparable contemporary masterpieces, such as Chaucer's *Canterbury Tales*, irrespective of some of the linguistic shortcomings or idiosyncrasies in the German texts. Wherever necessary, I have filled gaps in the original and added explanatory words or short sentences, each time using square brackets to clearly demarcate the difference between the original and my addenda.

Tucson, AZ, August 2006

No. 1
Jakob Appet:
The Knight Underneath the Baking Tub

This verse narrative has been preserved in four manuscripts from the early fourteenth to the late fifteenth century. The identification of Jakob Appet in historical terms is very difficult, if not impossible. We can reasonably assume that he originated from Zürich or its vicinity because of linguistic features, but nothing else is known about him. The anonymous author of the courtly romance *Reinfried von Braunschweig* from ca. 1300 refers to Jakob Appet as an alleged expert regarding women's lack of shame and their evil character (lines 15222-15225). Three of the extant manuscripts represent highly unreliable versions of Appet's narrative, and only the oldest, originally housed in the Strasbourg library, proves to be trustworthy. Unfortunately, it was destroyed during the fire in the library in 1870, and we have nothing but a copy created by Christoph Heinrich Myller for his *Sammlung deutscher Gedichte aus dem XII. XIII. und XIV. Jahrhundert* (1784).

EDITION

Klaus Grubmüller, ed., *Novellistik des Mittelalters*, 544–64.

TEXT

We have often heard what cunning and enormous tricks some women know how to apply, which allows them many times to avoid punishment by their husbands (5) whom they often trick and make fools of. To understand this, listen to the following story about how a knight experienced an adventure. I knew him (10), and he told me the story personally at one point.

He loved a married woman, and she returned his love ardently. They both were enamored of each other (15). Of their friendship for each other a thief might hardly have been able to rob them. Whenever it was possible they got together secretly. Never had a salamander felt better (20) in the hot fire than the two lovers when they were together. Their relationship lasted a long time, but at the end, because the guard never went to rest, something happened. The husband had three strong brothers (25). After they had heard so many rumors and had learned the truth, they immediately began to reprimand their brother: "May God rob you of all your honor (30), you truly bad guy."

Then they said: "Do you not know what people are saying about your wife, and that she is cheating on you? She loves a knight (35) who spends so much time with her that we all, who live here in this country, are dishonored." The husband answered: "This is not true; my wife does not love any other man (40) except for me, as I know for sure. She is so constant and so good, so I am convinced that she does not do it."

They answered: "But it is surely true (45), she has been having an affair with him by now for a whole year. Everyone in the city, that is, children, women, and all men, knows about it. Many people have kept it a secret from you." (50) Thereupon the husband said: "This grieves me. How do I find out the truth?" Then one said to him: "If you are willing to listen to us and to find out the truth (55), you should say tomorrow morning that you are planning to ride away. In the night you come back again, and allow us all to come along with you and guard all the doors (60). You yourself will go to the wall where you will be able to hear him speak inside."

The husband accepted their plan. In the morning, when it got light, he put on some of his best clothing (65), as also did his wife. He said to his wife: "My dear wife, let me entrust the house to you since I'll have to ride away from you (70). I got such news that I cannot ignore it, and I will not be able to return soon. So guard the house as well as you love me."

Thereupon the wife replied: "What are you saying (75)? You want to leave me alone? What do you mean by that?" Then she began to cry and spoke as follows: "You will commit a grave sin thereby, leaving me totally alone (80). Dear husband, stay here with me because I can hardly live without you." But she did not speak the whole truth. She was rather pleased with his departure and felt delighted about it (85). She hugged him with her arms and kissed him with her lips. However, this kiss did not come from her heart. She said: "My dear beloved husband, I will hardly be able to bear the separation from you!" (90) In secret, however, she thought: "Indeed, by God, if you were gone for a year, I would hardly care about it and would let the devil take care of you if I could enjoy love and pleasure (95) with the one whom I always enjoy seeing here." In his presence she shed many tears which had little to say about her true feelings, that is, her intense crying.

The husband would almost have given up his plans (100) and would have decided to stay home. He thought: "Truly, my brothers must surely have deceived me because they have lied about my wife." Then he said to her: "May you be well." (105) She answered: "I will not handle it as well as I am supposed to because your departure will pain me." He answered: "Take care, the time has come [for me] to ride away." This he did subsequently.

As soon as the husband left his house, she notified the knight right away (110) that he should come to her at night since her husband had left for a journey. He [the knight] would enjoy love and comfort. The knight: "The powerful God has blessed me," said the knight, and became happy (115). Soon he prepared himself in the evening and went to [the lady's] house. She was delighted about his arrival and greeted him in the name of God: "My friend and dear lord (120), now let us have a blissful life together since God has granted us a day at which my husband has gone on a trip. Do not worry at all that he might return soon (125), and you can believe my words."

For her friend she brought to the table much good food and the very best wine. She said: "My beloved lord (130), now live in great joys, now you are the master of this house, and whatever you wish will be done; no one will dare to oppose this. But let me tell you what is at stake here (?) (135), do not tarry, the time has come, the night is short. Let us go to sleep together."

The knight responded: "Let us do so, whatever you desire I will be happy with." Then they both went (140) right away to bed. There they began with a game which is commonly played on the other side of the Rhine. It was a game which the husband did not enjoy seeing. When they had finished their game (145), the lady said that her husband had departed from her without being angry with her, and that she had cried because of his leaving her, though she meant with that nothing else (150) but that she was happy about his departure. She told the knight all the details about her cunning, which was bitter for the husband to hear.

The latter had returned in the evening (155) and had [secretly] observed what they had done and said. His three brothers, who were with him, had listened to it all as well. They said: "Brother, do you hear him speaking?" "Yes, indeed, my brothers, I do (160). Unfortunately I hear him inside, unless my senses are deceiving me, and both, the man and my wife, will surely suffer bodily." The brothers then said: "Therefore, the time has come."

They began their battle against the adulterous couple and banged very loudly at the door. "O dear, for ever woe is me!" said the knight. "Where shall I go to hide?" (170) In response the clever lady said: "In the next room, where there is a fireplace, you can find a very big tub. Slip under it, that is my advice." The knight did not tarry (175) and hid underneath the tub naked. He would have preferred his helmet over his undergarment at this moment, as he later told me so himself (180). In the meantime the lady hid his clothes so that no one could find them.

While they both covered up, her husband outside called out angrily: "Do you not want to let me in?" (185) She shouted: "Yes, my very dear master." She opened the door immediately, and all four of them pushed their way in, trying to be the fastest, and looked in the bed (190) to see whether anyone was in there. But they discovered that it was empty. The bird had already flown away. The husband became very angry when he did not find anyone in the bed (195). "Light a candle,"

he then said right away. "Let me search in all the chests for the one who causes
so much damage to me, in terms both of goods and of honor." He began to turn
the entire house upside down (200). The wife said: "Why do you act like that?" He
answered: "You will suffer badly today if you plan to give me shit, you evil whore
(205)! For sure I heard your talking between you both when I stood near your
bedroom at the wall and you did not notice me. That's when I heard you talking."
(210)

She replied: "Let me tell you, I will lament this to God in heaven that you
have frightened me and woken me up so rudely. I was dreaming while lying in bed
(215), and I was filled with much happiness. I believed that I had you with me in
bed. Probably I then spoke some words, since I hardly ever get you out of my mind
(220). After all, whoever is wishing the best for another can hardly forget about
him, whether he is asleep or awake. If I have to suffer punishment for the fact that
I have such great loyalty toward you (225), then I will accept it as payment for
something that I have never enjoyed. And I might feel sorry for my loyalty and also
for my constancy because you have never found any lack of loyalty in me (230).
What do you blame me, a poor woman, for? I set my body as a guarantee for the
correctness of my claim that no wife has ever before loved a man so passionately
as I love you."

When the husband fully grasped the meaning of her words (235), he became
much mellower and let some of his rage go away. "May God protect you from all
suffering!" she said. "Dear husband, why do you act like this (240) against your
pure wife? May God avenge it on their lives who prodded you to hurt me and to
damage my reputation." (245) With her arms she embraced him and said: "Let
your rage go." Thereupon the husband: "All right." He immediately dismissed his
wrath. She [in turn] made sure that he did not find any person [in the house]
(250), and neither heard nor saw anyone. He said to his brothers: "The devil is
playing tricks on us. He who has often prodded people to commit murder cer-
tainly wanted me to kill my wife (255) and I would therefore become an object of
mockery. I will always thank God that the devil's evil force here did not gain its
victory." (260)

With these words the wrath was finished. The husband quickly ordered food
and good wine to be brought to the table. He and his brothers sat down next to
the fire and drank and ate. They made great noise, which caused the knight, who
was squatting under the tub and had little to enjoy, much worry (270). One of the
brothers sat on the tub under which the knight was hiding and said: "Now, we
have searched everywhere in the house up and down, except under this tub (275),
and indeed, I have not looked into it." He strongly tapped the tub with the fist. The
wife said: "This is inappropriate that you do not care to search also under the tub
(280) because he is, be sure about that, underneath it, I mean the one who was
with me in my bed. If there was a man with me in the bed, then you will find him

right there, nowhere else, because I told him to crawl under there (285) when my husband knocked at the door. I tell you the whole truth: if you do not search for him [in the tub], you are a coward." He began to laugh about it: "Do you intend," he said, "to make me a fool? (290) Tell me. I am not going to listen to your advice. We have been fooled enough." She answered: "But it is true, he hears everything we all have said (295); he is tired of squatting there for so long since he does not experience any joy. With the help of a courageous act he will have to be rescued from you, how badly you have thought about him." (300)

The husband said: "Dear wife, please let go of your mocking. If I had found him here in the house, your love for him would have turned painful for him, I swear by God (305); so spare us your mockery. I have been ridiculed enough, which was the work of the devil." In response the wife said: "I completely understand, my master (310), since mockery tends to follow an injury. You will be made even more a fool, as I would like to say openly." In the meantime it began to dawn.

Now, it happened that next to them (315) there was situated the house of a smart woman baker who well understood all matters that often concern beautiful ladies. She well knew the rules of love, and was intimately familiar (320), up and down, with what pertained to secret love; this was her particular skill. The lady knew well what pertained to love, whatever shape or form it might have. Everything regarding the rules of love was well known to her. This was the lady who owned the tub under which the knight was sitting and who intended to do a baking early in the morning (325) and make dough, for which she needed the tub. For that reason she needed to have her tub. She said to her maid: "Go there to the house of my cousin and bring me without delay the tub (330) which I lent to her last night and which I would deny to her very unwillingly."

The maid quickly went back and said: "My Lady, listen up, return the tub to us again (335), we need to have it tomorrow." The lady responded: "My dear friend, listen to what I want to tell you, let your lady know that it is spoken for, and that she needs to leave the tub with me considering our close family relationship (340), and lend it to me, which would be the greatest gift of love."

The maid went home again. Her lady asked: "Did you bring it [the tub]?" The maid: "No." The lady replied: "What has happened?" (345)

"Lady, she wants to use it better than for baking, and intends to apply it to a greater service if you let her have the tub [for the time being]." The mistress got very angry and said: "By all my honor (350), tell her to return the tub immediately, or everyone who lives in this street will hear about it, so I swear by the sweet Christ!"

The maid returned to the house (355) and said: "I must have the tub, Lady, believe me that." The woman replied: "Go home and tell her that a woman's emergency forces me to act. Do not say anything else to your mistress (360). I am sure that she will understand well that I am loyal to her."

The maid went back and said: "My Lady, rest assured, you need to forgo the tub for now (365), as I will demonstrate to you in all honesty since it means a woman's emergency." "My goodness," the lady said, "on the devil's death! Does my friend not need anything else? I am really surprised (370). If she had told me this before today, I would have freed her from her worries, however much anger fills the heart of my neighbor."

There was a little shed near by, just a little behind the house (375), and the woman baker set fire to it with a burning log. When the barn was in flames, she shouted out aloud: "Fire!"

What else do I need to tell you (380)? Many men came running toward it, and so did the husband with his brothers. In the meantime the clever lady made the knight escape from the tub (385) and let him out of the back door. She handed him his clothes into his arms and said: "Now it is up to God to protect you!" Subsequently she kissed him like a friend on his lips. Immediately the knight got away (390).

In this way the husband was deceived. This account is true, not based on lies. Women know many tricks, as Jacob Appet has told you. He who holds something under his control should keep it even better; if he loses something, what profit does he then gain from it?

No. 2
OF THE WISE ARISTOTLE; OR: ARISTOTLE AND PHYLLIS

We know nothing about the anonymous author, but based on his intellectual background, his thorough familiarity with Gottfried von Strasbourg and Konrad von Würzburg, and perhaps also on the linguistic features (Alemannic), it might be safe to assume that he originated from Basel or Strasbourg as well. Konrad von Würzburg died in 1287, and one of his narratives, *Herzmäre*, seems to have been composed shortly before his death. Since our anonymous author refers to that one, he must have written his *mære* sometime between ca. 1280 and 1300.

EDITION

Klaus Grubmüller, ed., *Novellistik des Mittelalters*, 492–522.

TEXT

Once there was a famous king in Greece called Philip. The story tells us that he wielded much power (5). All his life he was generous and noble. He excelled both in his body and in his manners, and stood head and shoulders (10) above the other kings in terms of power and wealth, as our source tells us. The blessed king had a wife who was so beautiful that it was said that no one had ever seen a more beautiful woman (15). Everyone who ever caught sight of her, from afar or close up, had to admit this. She was, as the report tells us, a flower of all womanhood (20). In terms of virtues she was beyond measure and as honest as the glass of a mirror, free of any fickleness and free of all evil deeds, as is the case with so many a woman's heart.

God graced the king and the queen (25) with a little child who later in his life conquered many lands. He was called Alexander, who was the highest-born child ever. No one who counts among the living today (30) ever achieved such lofty goals as lord Alexander did during his time. The child was, as I have heard told, beautiful and very virtuous (35). He displayed everything what one expects from a royal child. In order for him to study and to acquire a noble education he was sent to school. The king requested that a master be hired (40) who was wise and grey-haired because of his old age. His name was Aristotle. The king said: "Master, let me remind you of your honor and virtues (45); may you instill wisdom into the child during his youth, and teach it [well]!"

"I will do so," said Aristotle. He was so learned that his teachings have influenced the entire world until today and will do so for ever (50). He said: "I will teach the child according to the highest values and will provide him with insights (55) into all history concerning the world." The king said: "I will reward you well and will certainly give you many riches [in turn]." (60)

Outside of the royal palace there was a beautiful vineyard, and before that there stood a well-built house. [The king replied:] "Master, the house will be only for you and the prince, (65) along with the servants, whomever you would like to have around you."

They did not tarry, and the master took the young boy and taught him to read the alphabet (70), A B C D E. At first he had problems with it, as is commonly the case with children when they are forced to learn by a school-teacher (75). [But] then the young boy began to learn very much what the master taught him because his mind was able to absorb and to comprehend without any limitation. No other child all over the world (80) was more intelligent. Then, however, he was affected in his wisdom and in his reason by strong love.

The queen had a maid (85) who was, as everyone agreed, beautiful in body and appearance. Whoever looked at her was completely dazzled. Those who enjoy women's beauty (90) concurred that she was beautiful and praiseworthy. She descended from a high-ranking family and was a joy for the world. This delightful female creature (95) was a maid in the service of the queen, and was called Phyllis. Alexander began to burn because of the glow of her loveliness. The young man (100) was deeply affected in his mind. He thought about how the weight of his worries might be eased somewhat (105). He could no longer study; instead he thought of the maid. When he did not see her, he displayed great distress. Whoever is affected by love (110) would know how he felt. The martyr Alexander did not know what he should do. Love has never exerted so much force on a man's heart (115) in a thousand years as it did with Alexander. Whether he was standing or sitting, he always had in his mind the pure, good Phyllis (120). This lasted for so long that he, while the maid spent time with him, could develop a considerable intimacy with the lovely woman (125). Their minds were set on each other and both burned with passion. He was bound by love, and she even more. This went on for a while (130) until the tender virgin observed about him that he was crazy in love with her. Finally she promised him, since he begged her so hard (135), to go to a place in the orchard where she would await him. They both agreed upon this, which created friendship and loyalty among the two lovers (140). They enjoyed their love and happiness in full harmony whenever they could meet secretly (145).

Finally the master noticed about the young man that his teaching efforts had failed because of his love for the maid. This he observed (150) and so learned the truth. For this reason he punished the young man, who was mortally in love, hitting him, using reproachful words, and guarding him all the time (155), as much as it was possible for him. But this did not help at all: Whenever [Alexander] could leave, whether late or early, he went to his beloved (160) and enjoyed his time with her. The fetters that were to hold them both all the time broke because of their strong love (165). Their hearts and minds flew as high in the sky of joy as if they were eagles.

The master was badly chagrined about this development, so he went to the king (170) and told him the news that the young prince was lost to the beautiful maid. The king began to chastise the maid and questioned her about it (175). She said: "Sir, I am not guilty of the charge that he is raising against me. My Lady knows my character, which is so steadfast that I am not doing anything wrong!" (180) She swore so many oaths that the queen defended her innocence; and this reestablished her reputation.

The pretty Phyllis (185) was, however, still affected by love and desire. This robbed her of all her strength and happiness, especially because she and Alexander were so carefully guarded (190) that the pure and good maid never could get her heart's wishes fulfilled with him.

Alexander suffered from it (195), and he experienced heartfelt pain because his beloved was taken away from him. He sat on his school bench filled with wrath and growled like a bear. He turned back and forth (200). His mind was blinded by love.

The love-pangs also filled the young maid. The delightful and beautiful woman (205), who became very angry [because of the forceful separation], suffered likewise because the love between them had suffused her mind (210) and had forcefully undermined some of her self-control. She was no longer quite herself and showed a different behavior toward the world (215). Whatever had given her joy before and had been pleasant for her was now disagreeable for her.

Her whole life was now oriented toward a different goal (220). Her mind was filled with thoughts of how she, a sweet, pure, and good maid, could avenge the destruction of her love by attacking the wise master (225) who was grey from old age. Now listen how she carried out her plan. Phyllis, such a bright sun, went to a room, got a dress with a silken train (230), and put it on her delicate body. The sweet and lovely woman wore a shirt trimmed with fur underneath which was of high quality and made her look stunning (235). It was made out of ermine only. She looked pretty, believe me. On her head she placed a golden wreath, thin in its width, as was proper (240), created in a sophisticated manner, and jewels were embossed in it between the gems, very bright and yet small, the best one could find anywhere (245), emeralds and hyacinths, sapphires and agates. They were very beautiful and were attached to the wreath in a most masterly manner (250). Never before had gems been inlaid so artistically.

This beauty was well decked out. She took a clear mirror and inspected herself, her body and the color of her face (255), whether anything was amiss or needed improvement. She was really well-dressed, as we read in our source (260). She left the palace and went to the orchard, barefoot and adroitly; her legs were more white than snow, more straight than a candle (265), white without any stain. Her feet got wet from the dew. Nearby there was a fountain to which the maid turned, jolly and free of all cares (270). Her steps and her gait were well measured, neither too short nor too long, just right in every respect. She walked upright and openly (275) like a sparrow-hawk, and she was dressed like a peacock. Her eyes glanced around like those of a falcon perched on a branch, neither too softly nor too aggressively (280). And both eyes had their own pasture, and both hunted there skillfully and quietly, in a very sweet way. The lovely creature acted (285) like a wild animal, both in her mimicry and body language, yet still with proper moderation. She went back and forth; she lifted up her dress (290), exposing her legs almost to her knees. She began to pick flowers and put them into her lap.

Phyllis, who was as delightful as the sunshine, acted in this way (295) in order to tease the old man, who had robbed her heart of her love, and in order to deceive him. For this reason the lovely maid danced back and forth to the well like the bride of the wind (300) through the grass.

No one can tell all the tricks that women command. A woman can go hunting everywhere, and no one can be safe (305) from her cunning. No one is so wise or so grey-haired from old age that, if he wants to be with women, he will not be caught by the branch (310) and the lime-twig of love. This is the same case with the wild bird. When it is still free and lands on this lime-twig, and then wants to leave again (315) to fly toward the mountain, it is caught right there, irrespective of how much it might struggle. All the bird's efforts to free itself from the twig prove to be futile (320), even if it is very strong. The lime-twig binds it and holds it prisoner.

The same way many men lose in their effort and are bound by the rope of a woman's gaze when she looks into his eyes. It does not matter how wise he is or how indolent (325); no one can free his mind of women's cunning. If he wants to enjoy their company he might easily be caught (330). He who wants to be free of this danger should rarely spend time with women and should run away from them since there can be no other solution.

Now let us drop this topic (335) and return to our story, otherwise it might remain a fragment. The beautiful Phyllis played among the flowers—she was very confident (340)—and went back and forth. The old master saw this when he looked out of the window and observed her behavior. He liked her appearance (345) and recognized her loveliness. [He thought:] "How beautiful and how stunning, what a delightful creature is this attractive woman! Blessed the man who could grow old (350) together with her!" Afterwards he was suffused by chills and then by a rush of heat. Love put him into check and transformed him into a child (355). The lovely innocent maid reached the green lime tree in front of the master's window. There was nothing one could have criticized her for. She threw a whole bunch of flowers into the window (360) and called out to him: "Greetings and best wishes to you, and if I might be able to give you joy and a good time (365), I would walk for a mile, whether I were weak or not." The master said: "Many thanks, lovely, sweet fruit, all the world's happiness rests in you (370). Maid, be so kind and be open to the request of poor me, and come inside (375), we will be all alone." Thereupon the sweet and innocent maid, free of all blemishes, entered the master's house. It was her intention (380) to put him to shame, and this she pursued. She sat down next to him.

He said: "My mind and my senses have been pawned away (385). Though I have traveled through many countries, I have never seen such a beautiful maid. Grant me your mercy. I will give you twenty marks of gold and will take you to my treasury vault (390) where you can take as much as you wish!" She said: "Your words please me, master; what do you desire from me?" [He said:] "I want you to let me sleep with you for one night." She cried out: "Oh dear, and woe is me! Master, I will not do that and lose my virginity so foolishly." Then she noticed (400) that he was enamored of her like an ape. At that moment the lovely maid saw a saddle resting against the wall. She said: "I cannot do it without some reward (405). Allow me to put the saddle on your back; bear this and then let me place a bridle into your mouth (410), which will be my silken belt, and that's the way it has to be. I do not want to tarry any longer, you have to allow me to ride on you in the orchard (415). No woman and no man will see us there." The old man said: "I cannot well serve you as a horse." She replied: "But I want to ride on you (420) calmly and steadily like on a horse, for which I will then reward you and will do what you wish."

Now listen to this miraculous account of a young woman's cunning (425) against which there is no help. She was a lovely woman who had courage and was beautiful in her appearance. Hear what wonder she achieved and how much power she exerted (430) with which she could transform [a man's] heart and mind through her sweet words, although they are mixed everywhere with gall (435), and which easily defeat a man's skills, irrespective of how much wisdom he might command. Women's cunning creates wonders. Their flattering and cajoling, their lying in ambush and waiting (440), their speech and their singing, their dancing and their laughing, all this combines to make the rope and the bonds (445) with which they lead away the man with their own hands wherever they want. Women's skills are endless, as was well proven [in the past]. Adam and Samson (450), then the wise Solomon, indeed, the best men were all led astray by women. But Saint Gall [ironic allegorization?] tells me that women are not like that (455):

Women give joy to sad hearts that are weighed down by worries. If a man intends to have a dishonorable and unchaste relationship with a woman, this will not be possible because women are well guarded and free of all blemishes (460). There are thousands of women who excel in virtues. When a woman is free of evil, of an untrustworthy character, and of any blemishes, she also displays steadfastness (465).

Now let us return to our story where we left it. The powerful Lady Love, who mightily robs a man's senses (470), overpowered the grey master, the expert in the grand liberal arts. He said: "Beautiful maid, I am ready to subject myself under you, and I will do what you demand (475), if only you then grant me your love." The old fool went down on his hands and knees. The maid quickly grabbed (480) the saddle and put it on his back. Then she took her silken belt and put it into his mouth as a bridle. She had already plucked a branch full of blossoms (485) [for a whip]. The beautiful maid, free of all reproaches, took the bridle into her hand, sat down on this hero and rode him to her delight. She sweetly sang (490) a love song. Then the old man did not hesitate, he crawled on his hands and knees. This cheered up the maid's mind. He crawled toward the orchard (495), carrying the delightful maid on his back.

The queen, and many maids, caught sight of this. Standing on the battlement of the castle (500), the queen was greatly amazed that Phyllis gloriously rode in this strange manner. The queen delighted at it and was mightily surprised (505).

When the maid reached her goal, she happily got off the man and said: "You old fool, now you have been shamed for ever in revenge for having taken away (510) my honor and my love. With your hundred years of age you are not one bit wiser than a seven-year-old boy. The devil take you!" Gleefully Phyllis ran away through the grass toward the palace.

The rumors ran throughout the court, and the king and his people learned of them: The sweet and noble Phyllis (520) has avenged her sorrow.

Within a week the master packed his books and his clothing, and all his other properties (525), and sent it secretly in the midst of the night to a ship because he did not want to stay there any longer because of the mockery and the laughter and the unbearable disgrace (530) to which they subjected him there at court. The master went down the river that ran through the area into the valley because he could no longer bear the mockery and the hostility (535). He traveled far away to an island, called Galicia. There he stayed and wrote a good book, telling us what amazing tricks (540) can be employed by a distrustful woman, and how her life and body has hurt many a man. Whoever turns to women will be caught by them (545) like the fish by the hook, like the bird by the rope. Their persecutions and their glances catch men like the magnetic stone does.

I have reached the conclusion (550) that nobody can find help against it. Every man who enjoys his independence should stay away from them and run far away (555); nothing else is of use.

This little book should be known under the title "Aristotle." Pray to God with good intentions, then you might soothe (560) his bitter wrath, and your [soul] will never be lost; you will certainly go up to heaven. May the mother who gave birth to God help us (565) that this will come true. Amen.

No. 3
Dietrich of the Glezze/Gletze: The Belt

The narrative has been preserved in two Heidelberg manuscripts (Universitäts-bibliothek, Cpg 341, early fourteenth century; Cpg 4, ca. 1466/1478), and in a copy of the older Heidelberg manuscript, formerly in the library of the Kalocsa Arch-bishopric library, today in Geneva-Cologny, Bibliotheca Bodmeriana (orig. A1 XI; now Msc. 1). The poet identifies himself by way of brief references to a patron, Wilhelm, whose father was the administrator (bailiff, steward) of Weidenau in Silesia (today Vidnava in the Czech Republic, right on the border to Poland, al-most straight south of Nysa). This Wilhelm died in 1296. Since his father was most likely assigned to his post not before 1266, the narrative can only have been com-posed sometime between 1270 and 1290. Dietrich identifies his origin as Clezze/Gletze on the southeastern slopes of the Glatz Schneeberg in Silesia, although his language hardly shows signs of the Silesian dialect. He seems to have had a com-mand of Latin, and might even have been influenced by an ancient Greek source, the story of Cephalus and Procris, which underwent many adaptations and was even used by Ovid in his *Metamorphoses* (7. 655). Despite the reference to Brabant in the narrative, and despite the use of French loanwords, we know of no French source that Dietrich might have used for his own tale. But we know of an ancient Greek tale of Cephalus and Procris that reveals a number of significant parallels, although Dietrich borrowed only some elements and created an original tale after all: see Otto Richard Meyer, "Das Quellen-Verhältnis des 'Borten'," *Zeitschrift für deutsches Altertum und deutsche Literatur* 59 (1922): 36-46.

EDITION

Otto Richard Meyer, *Der Borte des Dietrich von der Glezze: Untersuchungen und Text.*

TEXT

I am called "The Belt" and should be known to honorable people, but unknown to evil people who should always suffer pain until the bitter end of their life because of their wrongdoing (5). This story ought to be read to a courtly audience which will be happy with me considering that they command so many virtues; after all, no one has to be reproached for his virtuous life (10).

Once upon a time there was a praiseworthy knight who possessed many courtly virtues. He was called Conrad and was well known in those days by knights and ladies (15). He spent much time together with the most noble people at court. He was very generous toward his friends and other people at court, and for this reason I would like to write about him (20). He pursued honorable goals, which gained him public respect: he strove hard through exercises to gain respect and ladies' love. One could see him often (25) stabbing and hitting, shouting out on the open field, and participating in tournaments in order to establish public reputation. Indeed, he was a splendid knight (30).

He had married a woman who had inherited many virtues from her noble family. Whoever was familiar with her knew that he had never seen a more beautiful woman (35). Oh, what a pretty person she was, how wonderful her body, her head with its yellow hair, and her cheeks with the color of roses, and underneath white as lilies! I am really amazed (40) that her eyes are so bright: she has eyesight like an eagle. Her beautifully-shaped nose was neither too large nor too small. Below she had rose-colored lips (45). Blessed was the person to whom she granted a kiss. Her chin was white and round, her neck was shining so white that one could see the color of the red wine when the lady drank (50). Her teeth looked like ivory, and her tongue was like a golden stick. Her shoulders were well formed, and she had such noble hands and arms as one could only desire (55). Her heart was filled with virtues. Whoever looked into her eyes felt the pain of love. Her whole body was well-shaped and pleasing (60).

Below her belt there was a gemstone which was clear and translucent. This was a miracle. My heart, tell us and sing of this secret thing (65)! It is a true marvel. Her legs and feet were shaped as was proper for courtly ideals. She wore elegant shoes. The palace where she lived was illuminated at night as brightly as the day (70). Moreover, I do not want to refrain from telling you about her goodness. It was so sweet that, if she ever stepped into seawater (75), then the sea would have turned good because of her pure feet and her white legs. But let's keep quiet about her feet. If they could realize her goodness (80), both animals and birds would have humbled themselves, and both the mountain and the forest would have bowed before her. Whomever she granted her greeting would not experience any sadness for three days (85).

Her goodness made everyone happy. Whatever knight might be married to such a wife would be blessed. She commanded extraordinary virtues, and never before had another woman been born more chaste (90. She never displayed any angry behavior toward her husband.

Once, in the blissful month of May, when all the other birds sing happily together with the nightingale (95), this lady was lying in bed next to the honorable knight, whom she loved just as a wife should do. He held her by her chin (100) and kissed her on the lips. He said: "My heart tells me that you are loyal to me. So far I have gained knightly honor [only] in foreign countries (105). Yet I do not despair, and intend to participate in a tournament to earn your happy laughter, and to serve your pure virtues which you have fostered since your youth (110). I have traveled through many countries full of joy and gained acknowledgment. Only in this country no one says that I am bold (115). I am entirely forgotten here. For this reason I want to participate in a tournament only two miles from here, and I would like to travel there soon (120)."

The lady said: "Yes, my lord, I will happily be at your service, now and forever." With this they concluded their exchange (125). The date for the tournament was set to be within two weeks. When these had passed—I am telling you—the knight prepared himself properly for the tournament (130). The lady blessed him, and he rode off.

When the bright day had reached noontime (135), the lady went into a garden for some comfort. Looking through the fence, she saw coming by on horseback a knight who was noble and attractive (140). His horse was fiery, and on his fist a goshawk [a bird of prey used for hunting] was sitting. With his other hand he held two greyhounds, truly shining specimens (145). He wore a belt which was richly decorated with gems. I tell you the truth. When he got clear sight of the lady, he felt a strong commotion (150). He fell so wildly in love that he almost lost his senses desiring her. He pressed the spurs into the horse and rushed toward the gate of the garden (155). When he reached it, he jumped off the horse and attached the horse's bridle to a tree. The two greyhounds (160) he tied to two branches; then he happily went to a bush in the garden and placed the valuable goshawk onto it. The lady approached him (165) and welcomed him politely. She said: "The weather is rather hot, but you escaped the heat, by God. Please sit down (170) until the bright sunshine relents some of its heat." She ordered a maid to bring wine in a cup and offered it to the knight (175). He was half-dead because of his love-longing. He drank in a well-mannered way and politely returned the cup with the wine to the brilliant miracle (180), to the wonderful lady. Love for her had badly wounded him deep in his heart. While they were waiting (185) until the intense heat began to fade, the beautiful hostess said: "Sir, I need to ask you, how do you dare (190) to stay here for so long? If my lord suddenly came here, you would irritate him (make him jealous) because he might wonder what you are doing here. But if you are part of his family through the bonds of blood (195), then it would seem to me quite appropriate that you remain sitting here. In that case I would know that it would be his wish that you enjoy a comfortable respite."

The knight said to the lady (200): "Good lady, you glory of honor, I am a foreign guest here; I do not know the host." Thereupon the lady responded: "Then you should ride off (205) and not stay here any longer." The knight replied in good spirits: "Oh, you are the promise of love, dear lady, I cannot go away from here. Your love has (210) put me into tight bonds." "She retorted: "Is this honorable when you think of how to diminish my honor? I really want (215) you to be quiet."

The knight kept sitting there without saying a word. Then he raised his voice again: "Oh, you valuable vessel [of love], good lady, allow me to live. I will give you a goshawk (220) worth five hundred marks. Don't be angry with me, a poor man; grant me, lady, what I am asking you for. Whatever can or should be able to fly (225), the goshawk [which I would give you as a gift] will catch."

The lady answered: "I do not want to gain a hunting bird for my husband in this way." "This grieves me," (230) said the good knight; "please fulfill my wish. I have two greyhounds that are so good that there is not one animal here on earth (235) which, if hunted by them, would, irrespective of its speed and strength, be able to get away. I will give you these greyhounds immediately if you untie the bonds of love." (240) The lady did not hesitate to reply: "For no dog would I throw away my honor and lower myself into shamefulness. No one will ever say (245) that a dog stole my honor. The words that you speak make me feel bitter."

The knight answered: "My lady, you heart-breaker, you sunshine (250), you noble fruit of pure manners, take command of me. I will give you my good horse which, when bridled, strives toward chivalrous honors (255). A gem lies in its chest which empowers it with strength and speed. It is a perfect horse in every respect. Whoever rides this horse will never lose the victory (260). It will be yours, but, lady, fulfill my wish." The lady replied intelligently: "You cannot win what you desire of me (265), I will not grant it to you. I will not sell my honor for a horse or its speed. A horse would not be enough to take my honor away." (270)

Then the knight spoke again: "My lady, you who are the blood of May, the joy for anyone who looks at you, you are the strings of my sweet love, you are the doll of summer (275); you catch me, miserable man, whom you have wounded with thoughts of love. Have mercy, you rose-lipped beloved! I have a belt which is decorated with precious stones on both sides (280) and with golden rings. One can surely claim that there are fifty stones, or more (285), some of which were imported from Morocco—this is true and not a lie. The black people from India and the people from Cytia [perhaps Sri Lanka] (290) brought them from beyond the sea. There are twelve valuable chrysoprases [green-dyed chalcedony], four onychites [a yellow alabaster], and three chrysolites [greenish-yellow olivine] embossed on both sides (295) of the belt. One stone came from Greece, which is known for its color. On the one side it has the color of clouds, and whoever wears it will notice (300) that he enjoys honor among knights. On the other side it is dark red and helps people out of many dangers (305), as I will explain to you. Whoever wears the belt onto which the stone is embossed will never lose honor and will always enjoy happiness (310); he will never be slain; he will never despair; he will always win the victory whenever he enters a fight. The stone helps against fire and water (315). If you let me have my wish, lady, the belt will be yours, and so will my hawk, the horse, and the dogs: just heal my wounds (320)."

When the knight had finished his speech, the lady looked down. She turned pale and then red again because of the gifts that he offered here. She called her chambermaid (325) and said: "My dear, make sure that no one comes here by chance, for which I will be thankful. Take the hawk and the dogs right away (330) and care for them, and also take the horse." Then she said: "Honorable sir, (335), give me the valuable belt, the hawk, the horse, and the dogs (335), which now belong to me alone." This made the knight happy. The lady said quietly: "Now your wish (340) will be fulfilled, without any doubt, with secret love. I promise you this truly." The knight handed over the belt.

When the lady lay down, followed by the knight, the trees rustled (345), the roses laughed heartily, and the birds sang loudly about it (350). Through the joys of true love the knight was healed from all his pains. Many roses sprang up out of the spot of grass where one lover's arms greeted the other's body.

Once the game was over (355), both flowers and grass laughed happily. When the knight departed, the wonderful lady said: "Now you have gotten your wish fulfilled, but you have profited little from it (360). You should have rather refrained from it. You have lost the belt, and also the hawk, the greyhounds, and the fast horse. You are out of your mind (365) that you throw away your properties so foolishly for so little joy." The knight responded: "My lady, do not say so (370). What you consider a loss, I consider my good fortune. I have never experienced so much happiness, lady, as I have here with you. Now, lady, show me your love (375) and give me a kiss." The lady kissed him lovingly. Afterwards he departed full of sadness.

A servant had observed what had happened in the garden (380). He rode to his lord and revealed the grievous news to him. He said: "Lord, I want to tell you, and I must lament by God, that my lady cheated on you (385). She had a secret affair. When I observed her, I saw in the garden a happy knight who did with her what he enjoyed doing (390). She fulfilled all his wishes." The lord answered: "Oh God, I have lost my joy! I thought I had chosen a chaste wife, but now she has forsaken. She has cuckolded me. Because she has shamed me so much I will abandon this country for good; I have lost my honor." (400)

He pressed his spurs into the sides of his horse, turned around and rushed away toward Brabant. The lady immediately heard this news which saddened her deeply (405). She said: "My lord is right in denying me his grace. I will have to

lament this. But while he is angry with me now, he will later change his mind."
(410) The servant who had betrayed the lady was chased away in disgrace.

The lady stayed alone without her husband, that is true, without knowing
(415) where he had gone. Whatever property she had under her control she man-
aged well. She planned everything carefully. She was courageous and bold (420)
and yet hardly twenty years of age. No one had anything [negative] to say about
her comportment.

When the month of May strongly chased away the cold April and put on new
leaves (425) and the forest turned green, the lady was filled with strong self-as-
suredness. She took five hundred marks but kept her plan secret. She said to her-
self: "My lord has kept a strong grudge (430) against me for a long time. I have to
go traveling to look for him, my dear husband, because I have never loved any-
one more than him." When the lady was ready for her journey (435), she took the
hawk on her fist and the two greyhounds on leashes; she put on the belt, and her
horse carried her joyfully (440). She left her home, accompanied by ten servants,
and was in a good mood. When she reached a beautiful city, far away, the good
lady (445) turned to an innkeeper who welcomed her politely. She thanked him,
jumped off the horse (450), and entered the house as a noble guest. The host or-
dered wine for them, which they drank happily. The lady spoke secretly to her
servants (455): "Now listen to me. Return home and protect my honor, keep every-
thing that I own in good order, and be loyal, you noble men." (460) The servants
said: "Good lady, whatever you want us to do we will be happy to carry out." Then
they returned home.

Now I want to tell you something (465). After four days had passed the lady
went to the host, took him by his hand, and said: "Please keep it to yourself what I
am going to tell you in secret (470). I am a knight, and not a woman, even though
my body seems to be weak. I have much strength if I want to show it. I had many
enemies (475) who threatened to overcome me. For this reason I put on this dis-
guise and came into this foreign land. Here, take four hundred marks, don't hoard
them (480), and resolutely hire twelve strong men and get each one a good horse,
armor and outfit. When I'll have such an entourage, this will raise my good spirits
quickly (485). Get me knightly clothing and splendid armor." The host got every-
thing for her, and even hired a jongleur (490).

What I am telling you is true. When the lady was properly dressed and had
cut her hair she appeared in front of the host in man's clothing (495). Oh, how it all
fitted her so well! Then she left for Brabant. When she got there and arrived at a
splendid castle, she ordered [her men] (500) to blow the trumpets, which echoed
all over. The duke heard this noise and said to his servants: "Don't be slow: I hear
foreign guests (505) who would like to enter the castle, and I would like to wel-
come them as well. Take a look to see who they are." A knight who had caught
sight of the lady (510) said to the duke: "It is a shining knight with an excellent

entourage." The host answered: "Let him in: he will be welcome in my house (515) together with all his squires."

They opened the gates to the castle and [the guests] came rushing in. The lady wore as her knightly dress a scarlet coat (520) with golden borders on all sides, embellished with a white feather; yet the belt that she wore (525) dazzled even more. A beautiful and lavish wreath adorned her uncovered hair. She would have withstood any comparison with other knights. The servants received the horses from the guests (530) and led them to the stables. The lady went up to the festive hall where the duke was sitting.

Her husband was also seated there eating. The lady was welcomed (535), but she appeared to be a knight. She was seated next to her husband, whom she recognized. He looked at her and said: "Sir, please tell me, what country are you from?" (540) She answered: "I come from Swabia." Sir Conrad replied: "Please let me know your name." The lady replied immediately: "Sir, I am called Henry." (545) Thereupon Conrad said: "You and I are foreigners here, and we should strike up a strong friendship which will help us in our knightly endeavors." (550) Sir Henry answered: "So be it, my dear fellow." In this way they renewed their old pledge of loyalty.

When the table was taken away (555), the hunting boys were called up and everyone went on a hunt, as our source tells us truly. They started to chase a bear, but the dogs' strength (560) began to fail in face of this wild animal. [At this moment] Sir Henry unleashed his two beautiful greyhounds, [and soon enough] the bear was overcome by the greyhounds' biting (565). The bear did not resist for long because he was bitten to death by them. They tore off his skin. When the duke saw this miracle (570) he thought that the dogs were strong, and he offered five hundred marks in return for the greyhounds. They were so fast that nothing could survive (575) that they were allowed to hunt. Sir Henry said: "My lord, I do not want to sell these greyhounds."

After the bear had been killed, they all rode out to another area (580) to go hunting with birds of prey, such as falcons, goshawks, and others. Sir Henry let fly his goshawk who killed forty birds. No other hunting bird there (585) was as good as he was. The duke was astonished [once again]. He offered many riches for the valuable goshawk, but Sir Henry said: "I do not wish (590) ever to give away my goshawk, as long as I live."

Then they rode home with great noise. They were all lined up on the open plain (95), and I am going to tell you the reason [that is, they intended to have a race]. Sir Henry rode ahead of them all. The duke offered him heavy gold and land for the horse (600). Again Sir Henry said: "My lord, the horse is not for sale."

Then the duke organized a tournament which was attended by many knights. There was also a proud Briton (605) whose armor shone in strong red colors, and so did his saddle cloth. His horse made leaps like a panther. He invited them all to

joust with him, but no one dared (610) to break his lance against the good knight.
When he noticed that, Sir Conrad jumped up in good spirits, put on his armor,
and stepped into the stirrups. He took his lance in his hand (615) and took cover
behind his shield. He rushed toward the Briton, but this was going to cause him
mighty grief because the opponent pushed him off his horse. Sir Conrad had never
experienced something so injurious (620).

When this news reached the court, and Henry heard it, he said: "I will with-
out fail defeat the Briton today." He was made ready quickly (625), when the duke
rode up to him and said: "Dear Sir Henry, I beg you with all my might, allow the
Briton to keep the knightly prize. You will be defeated by him (630); after all, he
has unhorsed the best one we have here at court. He is strong, whereas you are
not; you are not a match for him." Sir Henry said: "My lord, (635), please do not be
angry; whatever will happen to me today, I want to overcome the Briton." His ar-
mor gleamed like glass, and he was also protected (640) by iron leggings, which
consisted of tiny rings. His leg covers were of very good quality and red because
of dragon's blood. His sleeves were strong, decorated with gold (645). Around his
hips he had wound a silk cloth. A vest gleaming with light gave him a good ap-
pearance. His breastplate was covered with gems (650); his arms were protected
by metal vambraces. He wore a helmet with an excellent decoration, covered with
flowers the color of the month of May. He had an extraordinary sword (655) with
a most unusual scabbard interlaced with gold.

Now let me tell you of the belt which protected him from all suffering (660).
His vest over the armor was green, embellished with roses in gold color. In one
hand he held a spear, and in the other a shield which had a rim of gold. In the mid-
dle there was painted a white lily (665). An artist craftsman had made the saddle
blanket. The head cover for the horse was of gold, and the saddle blanket was
green, embellished with brilliant roses in gold (670). Because of the precious rings
the horse made a clinking noise. It pressed forward and began to jump. It neighed
loudly when it heard the sound of trumpets (675). Thus Sir Henry reached the
tournament field where the jousts began. Many trombones were blown. Sir Hen-
ry made a good knightly appearance. The Briton did not linger any longer (680).
Sir Henry broke his lance against him, and the Briton did the same against him.
Both then yelled: "Get me another lance!" When the lances were brought (685), the
warriors pressed their spurs into the horses and rushed toward each other full of
wrath, but the Briton lost because Henry unhorsed him (690).

Afterwards the tournament began in full force, knights stabbing and fight-
ing with each other. Wherever Sir Henry turned, everyone ran. The crowds of
knights (695) yelled loudly: "Attack! Attack! Go for it!" Sir Henry turned with all
his might, and the opposing group was completely defeated (700). With the help
of luck, which is called fortune, Sir Henry won thirty horses. Everyone praised
him loudly.

Not long afterwards (705) the duke organized a war campaign against a city. Sir Henry and Sir Conrad rode together to a guard post. Sir Conrad then asked Sir Henry (710) for the greyhounds and said: "If I would learn from you, my friend, that you would give me the greyhounds, or the goshawk or the horse (715), then the river of love would have flowed well toward me. If you grant me this wish, I'd thank you." Sir Henry said: "My friend, you ask for this in vain (720): I will not give you either the greyhounds, the horse, or the bird of prey; your request will not be fulfilled; you ask improperly." Sir Conrad said: "My friend, (725), please demonstrate all your trust. I will be your servant, and the chamber of my heart will house you with full love. Do not reject my request so harshly." (730)

Then Sir Henry responded quickly: "My condition is as follows: If you are willing to do whatever I want, then I'll give you the bird of prey." Sir Conrad answered: "My friend (735), whatever you wish, it will be granted." Sir Henry said: "My desire is a small matter: I love men, I have never loved women (740). If you do whatever I wish, I'll gladly give you the greyhounds and the bird of prey. But this has to happen secretly." Sir Conrad answered: "My friend, (745), I will have to lament this forever that you, wonderful knight, love men and not women." Sir Henry responded: "My dear man, now pay attention what I am going to tell you (750). If you do what I want, I'll give you the bird of prey." Sir Conrad said: "What is it that you want?" Sir Henry responded: "Listen, you have to lie down with me (755), then I will do all the wonderful things that I can imagine and think of, and especially what any man (760) usually does with his wife when he is lying next to her at night." Sir Conrad answered right away: "I will suffer everything (765), and not refuse anything, whatever you desire from me. I want to and have to accept it all in return for the greyhounds and the bird of prey."

With this they had reached an agreement (770). Sir Henry said to Sir Conrad: "Let us do it right here and now." He instructed Sir Conrad to lie down on his back. But then Sir Henry said: "By God, (775) what a loser you are! Are you willing to turn into a heretic in exchange for the dogs and my goshawk? You are a man without virtues! I am your wife in marriage (780). In return for the goshawk and the greyhounds, for the fast horse and my valuable belt which gives me knightly spirit in war and jousts, (786) I kissed another knight and let him sleep with me, so that you would gain more honor in knighthood with the help of the weapons and the strength of the belt (790). Now you are very willing to turn into a heretic in order to win my goshawk, whereas you had left me alone at home. You have brought shame on yourself! The wrongdoing that I committed was human frailty (795), whereas it was a crime against Christianity what you would have done voluntarily. You are a corruptible man considering that you would have abandoned, just for two minuscule gifts, your honor. I tell you, I am furious about that."

Sir Conrad said: "My wife, I submit myself to you. Please grant me forgiveness for my failure, my dear wife, you fruit of innocence." She answered: "I will be happy to do that, and I will also learn what your wishes might be; let us bury our anger (810). My lord, you know well that bore the greatest guilt. Now take the goshawk, the horse, the belt, and the dogs, which will guarantee your victories for ever." (815) Immediately afterwards they happily journeyed home to Swabia. From then on they closely guarded their honor and good manners in a most pleasant way (820), and lived every day without any worries until the end of their lives, when they reached the age of a hundred (825) without fail. This is certainly true.

Dietrich of Glezze has, with all his intellectual skills, created this poem for courtly people, and developed and structured it (830) as well as possible. Neither now nor ever after should anyone begrudge him this poetic composition, if he cannot create a better one. (835) Dietrich was always ready to serve ladies. He was always prepared to praise the purity of beautiful ladies. Alas, this habit is not practiced much today (840). The world has turned topsy-turvy: people strive only for material goods; they do not care about love. All people think only of money (845), which undermines the value of love which one should have for ladies. This does not please me at all. Whenever a man receives a wound in the depth of his heart (850) because of sweet love, he will not get well again through gold or glitter, but only through lips shining like red roses and if these grant him a kiss (855). This is such a sweet gain that he will lose all his heavy burdens. Nothing in all the rich countries can be compared with a kiss from such red lips (860). Blessed be he who can earn such fortune. I would prefer women's favor over silver and gold. No one can describe in words (865) the great joy which those receive from pure ladies who are in their service.

You men, I want to give you a lesson: you must honor ladies (870) and submit yourself to them because their red lips and their white cheeks liberate you from great pangs. All the pure ladies (875) will always be blessed. I am wishing them, from deep in my heart without fail and without hurt, that they will always be blessed.

William, a wooer of ladies and ever striving for virtues, (880) was responsible for me being composed. He never ignored any virtue. His father lived in Weidenau (Vidnava) where he was a high-ranking administrator. With this "The Belt" comes to an end (885). Grant your mercy, dear lady, to Punzinger, which will free him from his worries.

No. 4
Jans der Enikel[1]:
Sir Friedrich von Auchenfurt

Jans der Enikel (literally 'Jans the Grandson'), or Jans Enikel, identified himself as the grandson of an old family in Vienna, closely related to the powerful families Paltram and Graf. He lived between 1230/1240 and 1305 and composed two major chronicles, the *Weltchronik* (World Chronicle) and the *Fürstenbuch* (The Book of the Princes), the latter a chronicle of Austria under the rule of the House of Babenberg. The *Weltchronik* was created after 1272, and the *Fürstenbuch*, which breaks off in the middle of a sentence, seems to have been written shortly before Enikel's death. Despite his approach to his task as a historiographer, our chronicler/author was mostly interested in legends, anecdotes, and literary accounts, and less in factual reporting, and he hesitated little to adjust even the biblical account for his own purposes, actualizing it without caring much about the theological issues involving the typological function of the Old Testament vis-a-vis the New Testament. Not surprisingly, Enikel depicts the figures in the biblical narrative in the shape of medieval knights and ladies. The *Weltchronik*, which has survived in thirty-nine manuscripts, enjoyed considerable popularity and contains numerous verse narratives, including the charming, if not highly sentimental, account of *Sir Friedrich von Auchenfurt*. Enikel is one of the best attested persons in the history of medieval German literature and historiography, since we know of his family tree, his father's public role, his mother's residence in a convent, his children, and his job as city scribe.

---

[1] For an excellent discussion of this writer and his works, now see R. Graeme Dunphy's webpage at: *http://www.dunphy.de/ac/je/jehome.htm* (last accessed on August 30, 2006). For English translations of specific sections in Enikel's chronicle, see idem, *History as Literature: German World Chronicles of the Thirteenth Century in Verse. Excerpts from Rudolf von Ems Weltchronik, The Christherre-Chronik, Jans Enikel Weltchronik*. Introduction, Translation, and Notes by R. Graeme Dunphy. Medieval German Texts in Bilingual Editions 3 (Kalamazoo, MI: Medieval Institute Publicatiions, 2003), 17–24.

EDITION

Friedrich Heinrich von der Hagen, ed., *Gesammtabenteuer: Hundert altdeutsche Er-zählungen: Ritter- und Pfaffen-Mären, Stadt- und Dorfgeschichten, Schwänke, Wun-dersagen und Legenden* (1850; Darmstadt: Wissenschaftliche Buchgesellschaft, 1961), 3: 337–49; *Jansen Enikels Werke*, ed. Philipp Strauch. Monumenta Germani-ae Historica, Scriptorum Qui Vernacula Lingua Usi Sunt, III. Deutsche Chroniken und andere Geschichtsbücher des Mittelalters, III (Hannover and Leipzig: Hahn-sche Buchhandlung 1900) (esp.: *Weltchronik*); for a new electronic edition, pre-pared by Angus Graham and Graeme Dunphy, see: *http://www.dunphy.de/ac/je/je-home.htm* (last accessed on Aug. 30, 2006), verses 28205–28532.

TEXT

The emperor had a knight in his service who excelled through his many virtues. He was called Sir Friedrich von Auchenfurt and was a man of nobility. He was the most courtly man (5) the world has ever seen. He had been the lover of many very attractive women. A short while ago he began to woo a noble countess (10) who was so beautiful that he was most anxious in his mind to win the noble lady. But this truly beautiful woman did not want (15) to give in to his wooing. She said to him: "Sir Friedrich, be assured, if you do not leave me alone, I'll inform my hus-band about you." (20) He answered: "Whatever might happen to me, I will not abandon my struggle to win your love, or I'll lose my mind." He pursued her, this is true (25), for more than three years. Finally she pondered: "Oh, gracious good God, what could I do to this knight that he won't pursue me any longer (30)? I can-not force him to stop sending messengers to me. I wished I could bring it about in a proper manner that this [useless] wooing would begin to hurt him (35) with-out me experiencing further suffering from it. I might end up being killed by him just because I need to protect my honor. I am deeply troubled (40) that he does not stop asking me for my love; but I will never fall for him." These words she ex-claimed with tears, and lamented them in her heart. Many sighs she heaved (45) since she suffered much sorrow because of this knight, and this not only one time, but countless times. Then she conceived the idea of calling him into her private room (50) [where she spoke to him as follows:] "My dear sir, if I were to be your mistress in an act of adultery, I would lose my honor, and I am opposed to all evil behavior. Do you want me to be dishonored because of you (55)? I love you, my dear lord, with all my heart and my loyalty, whereas this [wooing] will be a pain for us for ever." She actually meant her own husband whom she loved full-heart-edly (60). She reflected: "I would rather burn alive than experience that I would ever be accused of evil as a result of my lack of morality."

One day the knight came to court (65) and secretly met the noble lady. Again he begged her for her love. She said: "What would you agree to do upon my demand [in return for my love]?" (70) Sir Friedrich responded: "Lady, rest assured, whatever it might be that you have in mind." The good knight spoke further: "I would be happy to be cut to pieces (75), and I would be ready to suffer the fate of being stabbed to death." Moreover, Friedrich said: "If I could enjoy your love, I would be your loyal servant." (80) The lovely woman responded: "If I am to grant you my love, you must serve me in such a way that I will be pleased with it." He answered: "Whatever you order me to do, Lady (85), I will do without fail." She said: "There will be a tournament here in the city, and I would like you to defeat many Romans who are anxious to win the renown of knighthood (90). If you prove to be the best, I will be ready to grant you my love. You have to meet a condition, however: if you can break many lances while wearing only your lady's shirt, and then joust against one who wears full armor and break your sharp lance against him, then, I swear to you, I will fulfill your wish (100). If you come out of this fight alive, I will keep my part of this pledge to you, however much I love my husband." The brave man responded (105): "If I can achieve this goal, betting my life and my property, I will be very pleased. I will go to this tournament [under these conditions], even if I might die." (110) She said: "If this will truly happen, honestly, I will not refuse to grant you my love."

When the tournament which the countess had mentioned was ready to begin, Sir Auchenfurt appeared there (115) and immediately approached a worthy knight, whom he selected [as the best] from the crowd, holding his lance, and asked: "Would you break a lance with me, noble sir (120)? Let us fight in the following manner: you are brave and not a coward, therefore I beg you in all sincerity to break a lance with me on behalf of your noble lady (125). But let me tell you of the arrangement: you must be armored in this fight against me, whereas I will attack you for my lady's sake without any protective gear. My armor will consist of nothing (130) but a woman's shirt. In this manner I'll be ready to joust with you."

The good and noble knight responded: "If I were to accept such a condition I would be a coward. If I were to wear armor and you none (135), this would be called a coward's way of fighting." But Friedrich, who was a truly great knight, answered him: "If I die here at your hand, as my lady has requested from me (140), I will forgive you, on my honor, and you will not have to mourn my death. After all, if I die because of my lady, what better could happen to me?"

He pleaded with the other man so much (145) that he finally agreed and went to the tournament field. They rushed toward each other as best as their manliness taught them. Sir Friedrich broke his lance most honorably, as everyone in the audience agreed (150). But the other knight was also successful and drove his lance all the way through his body, so that it came out behind him almost a foot long. Friedrich fainted and fell off his horse (155) onto the ground. He had to be carried off, and everybody lamented his destiny.

Now listen to what the countess said when she saw the knight lying on the ground (160): "Alas, you virtuous man, why have you thrown away your life and property for a lady's sake? You have sacrificed your honorable life for my sake (165). I wish I had never met you, which now causes me great pain because you are meeting your death because of me. Woe, you blissful man, could you not have offered your service (170) to another lady who could have rewarded you with her love? I love only my husband. You were such a stubborn man and therefore you lost your life for my sake, although I am nothing but a simple woman (175). You could have easily won a more beautiful woman than myself, which would have spared your life. Your death causes me great grief. Truly, you have suffered tragedy (180) and this pain only because of me. My heart deceived me [when I made this offer to you], and I will never forget that I love no other man (185) than my dear husband who will always be loyal to me."

Now let me tell you what happened to him, contrary to what everyone believed (190). He lay on his bed for more than a year until the sickness fled from him. The doctor threaded a hair from a horse through his body, which finally healed him like a horse (195) that had been wounded in a moss (?).

Once he was well again, he did not hesitate a minute to go to his noble lady whom he loved dearly (200). He brought with him the shirt that was all blood-soaked, which he had worn when he had been wounded. He said: "Lady, I am healthy again. Now consider, noble lady (205), what pain I had to suffer, and take into account, beautiful woman, whether I have not earned your love through enormous sacrifice." Then he presented her the bloodstained shirt (210) that he had worn when the lance had gone through his body.

When she caught sight of the shirt, she said with tears: "God the powerful knows (215), there has never been anything more painful. I would certainly grant you my love then if I would not be breaking the oath of loyalty that I swore to my noble husband. Is there not anything else (220) that I could do for you which would allow me to preserve my honor?" Then the good knight answered: "Since you are so steady in your mind and want to keep your honor (225), grant me then one thing, noble lady, that I would like to ask you to do, as I am going to tell you." She said: "My dear lord, there can be nothing so bitter (230) or so hurtful, unless I choose my own death, that I would not do it and which would allow me to preserve my honor."

He replied: "In four days the festivities (235) of Pentecost will be celebrated everywhere, as far as I know. Then you will do as I bid you: put on the shirt (240) in which I had been wounded. Listen to my plan. On St. Stephen's Day wear this bloodstained shirt, as I am telling you (245).[2] Beyond that, wear only a valuable

---

[2] In this context St. Stephen's Day, commonly celebrated on December 26 in commemoration of the first Christian martyr, means the Monday after Pentecost (see H. Grotefund, *Taschenbuch der Zeitrechnung des deutschen Mittelalters und der Neuzeit.* 11th rev. ed. Th. Ulrich [1891/1898; Hanover: Hahn, 1971], 100)..

veil, a coat, but no hat, and two new shoes. If you want to preserve your honor (250), then let the precious coat drop to the floor when you stand in front of the altar, visibly for me to see, gracious lady, since I will be standing in the choir (255). Wearing only this clothing, go and receive the Eucharist. If you do that, my lady, as I have told you, then you will be truly free from your oath; never mind what will happen to me." (260)

Thereupon the lady responded: "I do not care what this will mean for me, and even if it will cause me profound shame, I will do exactly what you have asked me to do (265), I promise you."

When Pentecost arrived, as I have heard, the lady put on the bloodstained shirt, just as Sir Friedrich had commanded her (270), and then a coat. She asked her maids to bring the shoes and the veil that she wanted to wear. Then she went to church (275), not forgetting her shoes. When she was in the church, her modesty granted her the crown of honor. She awaited the moment when the priest was distributing the Eucharist. When she heard the singing, two strong knights (280) led her to the altar [where she dropped the coat]. Indeed, this was grievous to the count [her husband] when he saw this with his own eyes. He was deeply dismayed and then thought (285): "Oh, good Lord, my wife has lost her mind: perhaps the devil has gained control over her; I would not swear an oath to the contrary." Quickly he went home, filled with fury (290). When she took the Eucharist, she let drop the coat made of silk. The shirt, which was totally soaked red with blood (295), extended down to her knees. Her good manners forced her to feel great shame. Then she put on the coat and went home, as her virtue told her to do (300).

The count could hardly wait for her to tell him the truth. He said: "My lady, tell me, have you gone crazy? How could you have done this (305) and dishonor yourself? What was the purpose of the bloody shirt that you wore in the church?" Then the lady told him the truth. Everything as it had happened she revealed to him (310). She did not hide anything from him and related the entire story to him. When her husband understood that she had suffered such great shame because of her steadfastness (315), he said: "Let me tell you first of all: I love you as before. But I have never experienced so much pain than at the moment when I saw you standing [in the church] without your coat on, and you were so beautiful." (320)

He pulled her toward him and embraced her. Full of joy he said: "My dear wife, from now on I will be your servant more than ever before."

Sir Friedrich left the country (325) when he realized the truth at that moment when he saw the beautiful woman standing exposed in the church. He was afraid that he might lose his life.

No. 5
Anonymous: The Little Bunny Rabbit

Translated by Maurice Sprague,
University of Salzburg, Austria

The text of this charming verse narrative was contained only in one manuscript, Strassburg, former Staatsbibliothek, cod. A 94 d. Johanniterbibliothek (ca. 1330–1350). Unfortunately, this manuscript burned in the fire of 1870, but copies created before that disaster happened have preserved the poem. Thematically it is related to the Old-French fabliau *La Grue* and *Le Héron*, and with the Middle High German *maeren Dulceflorie* and *Der Sperber* (*The Sparrow-Hawk*—here in our selection). Nevertheless, our narrative was created independently, though probably in direct response to or in conjunction with *The Sparrow-Hawk*. The anonymous poet wrote his piece around 1300 in the area of Strassburg and must have been familiar with Gottfried von Strassburg's *Tristan*, as the first line proves to be a quote from the latter text (line 41). Some scholars have argued that the first four lines of *The Little Bunny Rabbit* contain encoded the name "Gozold," but we cannot be certain about that at all. The poet might have been a professional goliard. (AC)

EDITION:

Klaus Grubmüller, *Novellistik im deutschen Mittelalter*, 590–616.

TEXT

If I should pass the time uselessly, since I am named akin to "God's grace," one would curse me. I wish, for entertainment, (5) to turn the tide against the envious, tell a little evening story, and weave an end to this rhyme in German (10). If I were so skillful and worked so purely that I needn't fear the slander of the envious hypocrites that are ready to criticize others unjustly (15) and wish that no other retain honor, then I would wish the indulgence of the nobles. And should Lady

Venus lend me insight, I shall leap[1] to give those hope whom one sees struggling for love (20).[2]

A knight, well mannered, who enjoyed the favor of the world, rode out with benignity and bravery through his land during the harvest when his people cut the corn (25), with two alert hounds and with a sparrow-hawk. This very hunter saw a young bunny rabbit (30).[3] He sent his two dogs after it and followed in hot pursuit. The rabbit was quick to flee and escaped into a field of rye; thereby its freedom was lost, for a harvester caught it (35) and gave it to the very same knight. That was righteous, God knows, for he had started the hunt.[4] This cheered the knight (40), and he thought to himself: "This is a really good start!" Then the admirable man considered what to do with it. His unwavering heart advised him to bring it to a young maiden (45) who had long refused him and for whom his passionate desire smoldered with hot longing, just as gold glows in the forge (50). He took this to heart; for one easily wins a child as a friend with such things: a child loves an apple, and would take an egg for the richest land (55). Therewith he rode toward a village through which his path led, following his sense of direction (60); he stroked his bunny constantly.

Now there was lying a young maiden, genteel, beautiful and graceful, in years a child and still naïve, in an arbor whose opening faced the road. (65) And as he rode in with the wild little beast before the tender young maiden, her eyes fell upon it (70). He greeted her; she said: "Lord, tell me, how did you come by the bunny? If only God wished it so and it was mine! Or is it perchance for sale?" He said: "It could very well be yours, beautiful child (75), if you are eager to purchase." "Yes, my dearest sir, I would very much like to have the bunny! Now tell me, what is it worth (80)? And if I have anything that you desire, which I can offer you, I will never have had such a glorious day!" He promptly replied: "I'll give it to you for your *minne*."[5] She responded: "'*Minne*', lord, what is that (85)? You are asking, God knows, for I don't know what! Take that which I have to offer, if you are inclined to pursue the transaction. Lord, locked in my coffer I have (90) three pounds of rings, ten dice, and a small belt of silk stitched with gold—my mother sewed red and white pearls on it (95) with all of her diligence and masterful skill— take that if you are in earnest, and let the transaction come to pass (100), for I have nothing better at the moment."

---

[1] Leap on horseback; gallop.

[2] Alternately: "I shall leap to fulfill her expectation (20) that one be seen fighting for love."

[3] I utilize 'bunny' or 'bunny rabbit' to help heighten the humor; a literal translation would be "hare" or "little hare".

[4] Literally: "...for he had hunted it."

[5] Minne: Love. *Minne* enjoyed a plurality of connotations and meanings just as 'love' does today.

The knight however replied: "Then the purchase can't take place; I don't want gold or gems, only your pure *minne*!" She said: "I don't have that!" He answered: "Oh, I'll find it all right (105), if I can search you for it." The maid replied: "So then take it; what are you waiting for? Give me the little bunny and take your '*minne*.'" (110) He said: "If there is someone around here who could hear or see us, then I can't take it; you have to be alone." Then the innocent maiden spoke, the gentle turtledove (115): "My mother is at church along with everybody else."

He then quickly dismounted and set the sparrow-hawk down from his hand (120). After hitching his steed, he lifted himself into the arbor and gave the bunny to the young maiden who sat there. God had forgotten nothing that makes a woman beautiful (125) when he had formed her. His artisanship shone in her form: her figure was flawless, her face was that of an angel, she possessed the virtues of a woman, (130) her modesty preserved her from reproach. She was so well built that even God himself would gladly see this young woman in his heaven.[6] And when this same maiden (135) received the bunny, she said: "Lord, I have what I want; take for yourself that which you desire." The knight did as he wished (140). He pressed the young child to him and kissed her rosy red lips as his desire bade him. Lord God! How he excited he became! Since the location presented itself to him, he laid her down gently, without uttering a blasphemous word (145), upon the blanket of love[7]—and her weaponry conquered him with aplomb—such arms have prevailed over countless armies and every king. (150) For everything—all that lives—struggles for love; love and lovely wiles have always held sway over the world. The young man found that to be the case here as well, and he enjoyed her sweet young body (155) until the maiden had become a woman. That seems to me, given my position, exceptionally wondrous.

And as the tender young woman (160) blossomed into summer, she said, "Search again, splendid hero—I don't mind— as often as you like until you find the '*minne*'; think of your bunny!" He renewed his search (165), and the maiden allowed it without dislike. Then he thought it time to ride away. The young woman, however, pressed him to her with the desire of her heart, (170) passionately to her breast, and besought him fondly that he not depart—otherwise it would be a sin!—before he found the '*minne*' at least one more time (175). But he feared that staying longer could ruin things, so he didn't delay. The young woman called after him: (180) "Lord, why are you in such a hurry? Why don't you take all of the '*minne*'?! I can tell, God knows, that you haven't taken it all! If you don't come back, I'll pity your loss!" (185) The knight rode away laughing.

---

[6] Double entendre with the meanings (1) 'in his heavenly kingdom', or (2) 'above him, partially obscuring the sky'.

[7] Literally the 'cloth of fasting', generally meaning the linen cloth covering the altar, though a religious symbolism might not be implied.

Now, her mother had heard mass and had come back. When the daughter saw her, (190) she ran up to her and said: "Look, dear mother, gentle mother, at what I have! A really cute bunny rabbit!"

She said: "Tell me, child, who gave you that adorable critter?" (175) She explained how she had paid for the rabbit, just as it had happened. At that the mother (200) began to pull her blonde hair and then to scratch her pale cheeks with her woeful fingers. The daughter was nimble and fled in leaps and bounds, eluding her mother's fury. She regretted the pain (205), but more that of being beaten than the loss of her *minne*. (210) With this in mind she went to the arbor every day and waited for the knight, believing that if he came again, she could take back her *minne*, and if he did what he had done before (215), that the would have her *minne* back, just as if the purchasing price hadn't been paid.[8] She swore to herself it would be so.

Now,[9] he came riding back (220) three days later. And the same moment she saw him, she called out quite loudly and said, as if she was quite out of her mind: "Lord! You should give me back my *minne*! (225) I have led a martyr's life, and it's been a sorry spectacle thanks to my mother! She tore out my hair! (230) I didn't do well to buy from you. Give me back my *minne* and take your bunny rabbit; we have to reverse the transaction. I have suffered enough since I lost the *minne*." (235)

Then the nobly-born knight said: "The *minne* that I took I shall return to you, if we are alone; may you regain favor therewith." (240) Now, the beauty ran down to him and brought the bunny rabbit with her. She said: "My compassionate lord, now that I am alone, take your bunny back and give me my *minne*!" (245) The knight was filled with happiness by the young girl's plea. Since he would have done it gladly anyway, he readily acquiesced (250). It is still the same today: whatever a man desires, he readily does it for the asking. In this way, a woman became a girl. Such a thing is rarely told; this is what I mean, so take note (255): she believed to be as she once had been, a virgin once again, although she didn't fit in virgins' ranks. Who would doubt this tale (260) that the good knight benefited from her pure *minne*? No one should disapprove of that, or of the adventure that the story tells us.

The golden gilding of Love (265), now who earned her blessing? The blessed knight! Because the lovely girl believed she was a virgin once more, as she once was, (270) something she had already lost. And as this adventure unfolded, the maiden looked with great frequency at her most cherished bunny rabbit. And he demonstrated his chivalrous sensibility in that he gave her back her *minne* (275), and afterwards also let her have the bunny. That was her victory. She thought to herself that she had managed quite well (280) and that he had been fooled.

---

[8] Literally "...hadn't been lost."

[9] I translate 'nû' as 'now' to emphasize the narrative quality of the text.

Then, as the knight prudently rode away on his horse over the fields, the mother arrived. The girl appeared and ran towards her straight away (285), and she called out quite loudly, more than twice: "Now, mother, I am healthy again! The knight was here and gave me back my *minne* and even gave me the rabbit (290) as a present!"

The mother screamed: "Cursed be your recovery as a 'virgin', and curse upon your gain [of the rabbit]!" In her despair she tore at her daughter's hair (295) and then she said: "Now I know very well, insofar as I am your mother, he took your virginity. I will have to regret that forever (300). Alas, my child! Your reputation! I should have watched over you better; then I wouldn't be in this miserable situation, in which my heart is to be buried so long as we both live!"

"Come now, cheer up, it happened (305). You should look on the bright side," said the ignorant girl. The mother answered: "My misery continues without letup, and shows me how I shall perish!" "Dear mother, be consoled (310). I did it and should live gladly with the consequences. Hush, and leave off your pitiful yammer."

The consolation of the child had an impact on the mother. She said: "I still might live to experience pleasant days and joy with you! (315) Happiness will not be denied you. Let it be, put on your wreath [of virginity] proudly; you aren't washed up yet! Be quiet and let it be seen that you are happy; a miracle may yet come to pass." (320)

Over a year later, the knight was publicly engaged to a young woman who was to be his wife. She was beautiful and intelligent (325), well-bred and rich enough, and wore the virgin's crown, according to which she was supposed to be a virgin: such a circlet is the privilege of virgins (330). The loyal knight of honor expected nothing but good to result from this marriage. For that reason he was happy and took on the costs and expenses. He began to invite lords and ladies who were his friends (335) to his country for the honorable wedding. Now listen to what I believe: that which should happen, happens (340); that is what I believe, and nothing else. That was demonstrated in this very case: it happened as it should.

The worthy and fine young knight thought about his bunny—and about the cute girl (345)—and the story about how the transaction took place. His noble heart couldn't let it be; she had to be at court (350), his maiden and the bunny rabbit. Oh, he should have left her at home! He promptly rode out to where the affectionate purchase had taken place. The maiden was the first to see her friend that she carried in her heart (355). She called out: "Dear mother, look! There he is! The one who took my *minne*!" The mother was quite taken aback. "Oh, child, why did you remind me!" (360)

Now, he had approached and bade the woman, her mother, that she attend his wedding out of respect for him, and that she bring the maiden and her bunny (365). She thought: "Oh! My reputation! If I go to the wedding of the man who won my

daughter as a mistress, how little joy I will have when I look at him (370), since he
rightly should get married to your daughter, if he were only willing. But I very much
fear, if I refuse, that he will reveal the whole story." (375) So she didn't want to refuse
him. "Gladly, lord," she said, "I am pleased to be so honored by you. We should both
be glad to come." (380) Then this exceptional knight said: "Blessings and thanks
forevermore; I will never forget your kindness!" He very happily departed for home.
Now, as it came to pass, on the day of joy (385) on which his wedding was to take
place, he sat fondly at the side of the woman who was engaged to become his wife
when—miraculously—in rode (390) the naïve young girl of whom I have told you
already, and she brought his cuddly bunny with her, without any guile. The host,
who very well knew how the bunny had been bought (395), and how the daughter
had been punished, and how the transaction had taken place, chuckled and gave a
guffaw and then began to laugh so uncontrollably hard (400) about the whole affair
that people wanted to help him. He finally got a grip—just barely. Many wanted to
ask why he had laughed so much (405), but the honorable man avoided answering.
I guess he didn't want to share his secret with anyone else.

Then the young woman (410) who was to be his bride began to ask in earnest
why he had had to laugh so heartily. He didn't want to give the affair away, and
told her to stop asking (415). Curiosity gripped her all the more, and her questions
were more urgent than before. She really wanted to know (420) where all this jol-
liness came from. He fended her off: "Don't act like that!"

She said: "You tell me this story, or, by life and limb, you will never have a good
wife in me or a pleasant day." (425) The woman's threats tipped the scales, and he
told his tender young bride in accordance with her desires (430) that which she
wanted to know; he told her of the rabbit hunt, how it escaped into the field of rye,
how it was later sold, how the daughter was punished because she lost her *minne*
(435), and how he enjoyed her yet again when he gave the *minne* back to her. She
said: "In the name of the Holy Sepulchre! She was a fool (440): if she had had my
prudence, God knows, she wouldn't have said anything! That was really stupid.
Ha! In truth, our chaplain did the same with me a good one hundred times, and
God knows I would regret it to this day (445) if my mother found out about it. Ha!
What a complete fool! Why didn't she leave off blabbing?"

When the knight heard this (450), a terrible fear struck his heart. His color
changed so drastically that he could hardly sit, first pale and then red, as his fear
would have it. When he came to his senses again (455) he began to consider what
had been said. He thought: "If that's how it is, my marriage will be consummated
(460) quite differently than I thought!" He didn't remain seated, he leapt to his feet
in anger; in a huff he went over to the maiden that had come with the bunny. He
sat her next to him (465), she whom he had originally greeted with mockery. Eve-
ryone who had come, all who had gathered there, men and women (470), believed

the young woman to be the fiancée.[10] The host rose, as I have heard, and bade them all listen; he told the story from start to finish, in measured words, how it had happened (475), about this and that, and how he purchased the maiden and took away her *minne* and how he gave it back to her (480). After that he told them about his actual bride and her chaplain.

And when he had told the whole story, he hastily asked his friends (485) who were there to tell him, in the spirit of friendship, which of the two they would unanimously approve of (490), so that he take her as a wife. They then advised, with a unified voice, that he should rightly marry the young beauty with the bunny rabbit (495), if he wanted to pursue what was correct and honorable. Then he waited no longer, he took her with a wave of the priest's hand.[11] The other one was sent back home to her chaplain (500).

I still have faith and believe and will always claim that what should be, that has to happen. Just like it happened and was publicly demonstrated (505) in the case of these two women.

---

[10] "... believed to have found a bride in the engaged maiden."
[11] "... with the hand of the priest."

No. 6
Ruprecht von Würzburg:
Two Merchants and the Loyal Wife

As in most other cases, the author of this verse narrative, Ruprecht von Würzburg, is not identifiable through any references to him outside of this tale. According to his own testimony, Ruprecht originated from Würzburg, but it is not certain whether he also lived there—as we know from Konrad von Würzburg (ca. 1235–1275). But his language is Franconian, and the tale was obviously greatly appreciated by someone close to the notary public for the Würzburg bishop, Michael de Leone, famous for his collection of a wide range of literary, didactic, and factual texts. The unknown scribe copied Ruprecht's narrative into a manuscript today housed in Gotha, Forschungsbibliothek, under the call number cod. Chart. A 216; the text is contained on folios 76vb–82rb. Ruprecht seems to have composed his text sometime in the first half of the fourteenth century.

EDITION

Friedrich Heinrich von der Hagen, ed., *Gesammtabenteuer*, 3: 351–82.

TEXT

I am acting like the fools who bring to the ears what has been put into their mouths, whether it is evil or good, and let it rush out of their mouths (5) as if they had been asked for it. Likewise I, foolish man, am doing it as I am beginning with a weak mind to tell you a story (10) which is too difficult for me. It is a *mære* [verse narrative]. I am afraid it won't be perfect since I have taken on this task. After all, I am void of good sense (15) and filled with foolishness. Therefore I am asking you all, whoever is going to be displeased when he hears a reading from this little book, to have mercy on me (20) and not to criticize my account composed in verses. After all, I do not do this often. May God send me His help so that I can complete this *mære*.

In France (25) there is a very rich town called Verdun, well known among merchants. In this town lived, free of all dishonor, the most respected men in the country (30), two merchants. Both felt great liking for the other, with upright and steady hearts. Constant friendship (35) fully ruled in their hearts. They pursued this virtuous relationship for a long time. Each of them would have been ready to risk for the other their life, their property, honor, and family (40). One of them, however, was very rich and had reached, with God's help, a much higher rank than the other. He was called Gillot. The other stood in his service (45), as if he were his liege-man. He served him free of all shame. His name was Gillam. He had a son called Bertram.

Gillot had a daughter. He could never let an hour pass without having visited Gillam out of friendship, sitting down with him, or standing around deliberating with him (55). He was compelled to do so out of love for him.

His daughter was called Irmengard, and possessed beauty and virtues. Sir Bertram (60) was free of all evil and strove for virtue. For this reason he was praised far and wide. But his fortune [during his life] was not all perfect and well-rounded.

The two old men (65) had complete control of the city. No one could oppose them. Sir Gillot thought much about how to guarantee that he would honor Gillam (70) with so much friendship that their bond of loyalty would, because of its strength, never come apart. He believed that it would give full confidence (75) to the entire city when there would be no conflict anywhere if their two children would marry (80). He pursued his goal, deliberating it much all day long. One night, after having kept these thoughts to himself without telling his wife about them, he decided (85), when they were lying in bed, not to keep it a secret. He told her what he had in mind and said: "My dear wife, I have conceived the idea (90) to give Irmengard to the young Bertram, the son of my friend Gillam, as his wife, which would provide us with much happiness, and [our families] would rule well together." (95) She responded: "Lord, do not say so. What crazy idea is that? Where have you lost your mind, lord? Let us forget your words, they make me quite angry (100); you are half mad."

Gillot then replied and said: "Wife, why do you act like that? Do not speak thus and try to understand me a little (105). You are confused in your mind, I know well what you would like to have [as sons-in-law]: counts and dukes, indeed, that is not a lie, have asked for our daughter's hand (110), hoping that I would agree to their proposals. I will always strive against this strategy because it would give me great heart-pains (115) if my daughter were to be mocked like a cow because she is not aristocratic. Listen to my idea: my daughter is to take [as husband] a man (120) who will be fitting for her."

His wife said: "What you want, that will be done." When she said these words, her husband replied, full of love: "May you be blessed, my dear wife, (125) for complying with me in every respect. For this reason I must love you until the end of my life. You possess such good manners (130). Let us not wait any longer and begin with the preparation to achieve our goal; I would like to reach an agreement by tomorrow morning."

"Yes, my dear lord, do that," (135) [she said]. Soon thereafter dawn came, and the man did not tarry. He went to Gillam and asked: "Where is Bertram? There is something that will make him happy (140): I want him to marry my daughter because I like no one better, by Christ, than him to be my son-in-law."

Gillam responded: "Lord, please do not do that to me; why do you mock me, a poor man? (145) I have always served you loyally; allow me to continue doing so, and if you do so, you will do well. I deserve this, and then I will give my best service to you." Thereupon Gillot answered him (150): "I am serious, this is not mockery. What would I have done with my reason if I had the intention to mock you? No one will be able to change my mind, and you should send for your son." (155) Then both swore an oath [of friendship?].

When the young man heard of this, he came rushing to his father; and soon also lady Irmengart appeared, who was pledged to the young man (160) as his future wife. He embraced the beautiful maid and pressed her tightly to himself, as I have read in my source. The maid cried loudly (165), which demonstrated her chastity and her good female manners. It would have been considered a failure of custom to hear that a woman had not been frightened (170) when she was about to be married to a man whom she had never considered as her bridegroom, and then in that situation would have remained dry-eyed.

Without any delay they organized for Bertram a wonderful wedding (175), and a better one had never been seen before or ever since. Unless anyone tells it differently, I will not question this claim. Then the sun was setting (180), and the evening star (Venus) rose according to ancient customs, if I have been told the truth about it. The two young people were welcomed by a bed, and much love happened there (185), and so a lovely embrace. — It seriously irritates me that my thoughts are led astray so far, but unfortunately, this is the case. — Let us keep quiet about the rest (190).The young man and the most beautiful maid found each other, he kissed her more than a thousand times on her rose-colored lips.

The night came to an end, filled with joys (195). The lady and my lord Bertram took each other's hands and walked to a hall filled with the loud sound of happiness. There people played drums and violins, (200) also flutes and some stringed instruments. Many women joined in with singing. Afterwards tablecloths were brought in to set up for dinner (205). Servants covered the floor with flowers and green grass. All the noble guests in the palace had washed their hands with water. Then one could see (210) the stewards and cup-bearers arrive, who would not dare to waver in their duties. They offered their best service and much more, whatever any guest could think of (215). The host did not want to spare anything and withhold any of his goods. He had a noble character: the best person acts accordingly in the best manner.

After the wedding had come to an end (220), the young man began his life at home with his very beautiful wife whom he loved more than himself. She loved with equal strength. Neither previously nor ever since (225), in fact at no other time have there been two people so much in love with each other as these two were. They experienced no conflicts between themselves. Whatever she wanted, he also wanted (230); whatever he liked, she liked as well. So they could not help but to live in pure bliss. God had fulfilled their wishes and provided them with a paradise here on earth. There has never been a poet so wise (235) who could have fully described in poetic terms the bond of love between them. I am fully aware that it could never be torn apart (240).

What I am going to tell you is the truth. The husband took good care of his house in every respect for ten years, listening closely to good advice. In this behavior he was followed by his wife Irmengard (245) according to her special female qualities. No other woman displayed more stability based on complete virtue because she was the root of honor.

This man, my lord Bertram (250), increased his wealth through his activities as a merchant. By contrast, those who do not add to their capital and want to take away from it will experience a hard life or will lose everything (255). One day the young man prepared himself for the yearly market in Provins. He was smart and wise in many different mercantile matters, and therefore he possessed taffeta, spices, raw silk, and violet cloths, and many highly valuable clothes. With these he went to the various fairs and offered them there for sale. This made him exceedingly wealthy.

He said good-bye to his lady (265). Great anguish filled her heart because her sorrowful mind told her—as often happens with me as well—that he would stay away for too long a time (270). The young woman shed burning tears; she embraced her husband and kissed him intensely. She said: "My dear beloved husband, whom do you plan to designate as my guardian? (275) Since you want to leave me, my heart is weighed down heavily with much sorrow and it has to be plunged in great worries. All my joy will be robbed from me (280) until you come home again." The husband's eyes began to turn red, which was caused by his own great love for her. He said: "My lovely wife, why do you torture yourself (285) and why do you make my mind so heavy? The dear God will protect you for me! Do not doubt it at all, I will always be loyal to you. I will return in a short while (290), if God grants me good health. Your sorrow lies in my heart."

Then the young man left and traveled well over ten thousand yards to the city of Provens (295). He immediately asked to be directed to the best innkeeper who would be the most experienced to host a guest. He was then taken (300) to a wealthy innkeeper who welcomed the very young guest in a friendly and courteous manner. He came up to him politely and greeted him in God's name (305). The young man said: "May God reward you, my lord: let me have a room where I can store all my goods without facing any danger and where I can manage them all by myself." (310)

The innkeeper complied with his request. He ordered the best quarters he had to be immediately readied for him and for his wares to be stored there. Bertram was very pleased about it (315). Once this had happened, the guest was asked to come to the dinner table in a wide dining hall, which was filled with rich merchants (320).

When the meal was over, the innkeeper asked his guests to be quiet and appealed to each of them to tell a story about their wives that would illustrate what character she had (325) and how she lived in her house. The first said: "Well, oh well! My wife is a terrible horror, she is a devil and not a wife. And if all the devils from Hell were sitting on the threshold of my house, none of them would dare to approach her." The next merchant said: "We have well understood what you have reported to us. But I think that you commit a sin (335) against your good housewife. Mine does not behave like this toward me, instead she is happy and virtuous as soon as I leave her. She takes pity on her fellow Christians (440), which is praiseworthy in the eyes of God: therefore I am raising two bastard children." The third one spoke thus: "That may well be; my wife is better than any merchandise, and she is characterized by constancy (345). Moreover, she knows a trick which is better than those mentioned before. She drinks so often that her speech becomes slurred. In this way my wife (350) takes care of my house and all my property."

Such stories they exchanged among each other, and none abstained from casting blame on his wife, whereby they hurt their own honor (355). The young guest Sir Bertram silently listened to their talk and greatly praised God for all the honor that He had bestowed upon him (360). Then the host addressed him in friendly fashion and said: "How come, sir, that you do not entertain us with a story about your lovely housewife?" (365) The young man responded: "So be it. At home I have a pure wife whose very lovely appearance often makes me happy. My heart is full of joyful laughter toward her (370). When my eyes are looking at her, no woman ever felt more love toward her husband than she. She excels through her womanly virtues: chastity and a pure mind (375); moderation and real grace follow my wife, and so do self-discipline, wisdom, and proper manners, and she behaves nobly. She is the crown of all praise (380), and this crown she wears with full justification. More I cannot tell you about my wife's reputation. She is the flower of all women and the Easter of my heart (385). I cannot compare her with anyone. She is the praise of all women, and her dignity even exceeds her virtues."

The innkeeper said: "I observe that you must be raging mad that you want to give so much praise to your wife." (390) "No, indeed," said the young man, "she can identify and judge all the good things properly. Never mind how many virtues I might mention, she still commands many more." (395) The innkeeper responded: "You had better follow my advice, and do not give her so much praise, otherwise you will lose some of your honor that you believe you can claim. You do not pursue a smart approach (400). I bet you that I can go to bed with her within half a year, if you dare to wager indeed for everything that I owe (405), if I have permission to try it. And if you don't mind, then pledge everything that you owe in return. If you lose, you will from then on (410) have nothing but the shirt on your back. To match that, I wager all my property, which will be yours in the opposite case. Whoever loses will be obligated (415) to turn over all his goods that he previously owned or might gain in the meantime to the other, based on sworn oaths. Let us maintain this pledge, even if one of us might regret it (420), so that he cannot withdraw from the wager."

This pledge was immediately sworn, and none of the two was inclined to withhold it. The innkeeper asked the guest to stay there and to send a messenger to his home (425), telling his wife that he had decided soon to travel to Venice without delay. The messenger should also tell his wife to treat his servants (430) in a fully honorable manner since they had always been dear to him.

When she received this news, the joy in her heart was badly destroyed (435). Her heart was filled with sorrow and pain. Her cheeks were covered with the rain of her eyes' tears. She exclaimed: "May the true God's blessing always protect him! Why does his manly goodness not grant me consolation? Oh, my heart-beloved husband, will I ever see you again? (445) I am longing for your return, yet I have to forgo this for now." But the woman found consolation and maintained the house in a praiseworthy manner.

As I have told you, the innkeeper had arrived in Verdun. This proud man, [named] Hogier, was intelligent and cunning, so he found a place to stay across from the lady's house. Whether she went in or left the house (455), wherever she moved, he acted accordingly, so she had to give him regular greetings. This inspired him with good hopes (460) because he was very happy [about this development].

He thought to himself: "I will arrange things for sure in such a way that I will win his property and his wife. For this purpose I must dress up well in order to acquire both, otherwise I will fail miserably (465) if I do not succeed in this wager."

Both at night and during the day he strove very hard to figure out how to achieve his goal (70). He began to send little gems and many greetings to the woman. But she threw everything on the floor and stepped on it, filled with great disgust (475). She had him told in all earnestness that she would complain about him to her relatives, which would destroy all his plans.

As this plan failed, and this bait did not work (480), he went to her servants and bribed them heavily, making sure that they were thinking of him when they would sit with their mistress. Then they should speak to her about him (485). He emphasized: "I'll be deeply obliged, I promise, and if you help me to achieve my goal, you can count on me to receive a great reward, which will ingratiate you to me for ever." (490)

Once this had been arranged, the servants began to give high praise about the merchant [the innkeeper]. The lady said: "Children, are you crazy? If you want to sell this man, then seek out another merchant. I have no intention of buying him. I will never accept him for money. Stop your talking altogether, or I will give orders for you to be (500) badly spanked." Immediately they were all quiet about him, changed the topic, and lowered their heads as if they had sneezed (505). They never mentioned this matter again and kept quiet about it.

When Sir Hogier heard this news, which was very bad for him (510), he lost all joy. Since this strategy had failed and did not work at all, he thought of a new plan. He thought: "I must achieve my goal (515) in a short while, it does not matter at what cost." One morning as he was walking to church, he took aside one of the lady's chambermaids, the one who was her favorite (520), and said to her: "No poet has described such love pangs as I have to suffer. I will surely be a dead man if I do not win your lady." The maid was called Amelin (525). He said further to her: "Would you like to earn some money?" She answered: "I would not be opposed to it." So he put a pound of silver into her bodice and offered her even more reward [if she complied with his request] (530). He said: "Offer your lady possession of my goods: she can take as much as she would like, and I would not want to be miserly toward her. In fact, I would like to give her a hundred marks (535) if she grants me my wish." "I'll be happy to do so," said the maid Amelin, because she was anxious to get the reward, and continued: "The power of good fortune shall be in your hands (540). I will go to my lady and let her know what you said."

[But the lady retorted:] "Keep your mouth shut and never even think of it, or I'll arrange it that you will be severely punished (545). I possess enough money; I will not sell my honor."

As this plan had not worked, Hogier immediately offered two hundred marks (550). But the lady did not care for it a bit. This increased his worries. The time agreed upon [with Bertram] came close. At last he offered a thousand marks to the lady (555) in return for enjoying one night with her. Amelin said: "What do you think? Don't you want to earn this money? You act very badly toward my lord (560). Certainly he travels through many countries, but he will never have the good fortune of winning so much money; dear lady, think about it and change your mind (565) if you do not want to arouse my lord's anger." Her lady Irmengart answered her—and no woman had ever shown more loyalty—: "Do not say one more word. I will complain to my relatives (570) who will give you a harsh beating." [*The following section consists of highly idiomatic formulations that can hardly be translated, hence I am using an adaptation.*] The maid said: "Do as you wish, I would not blame the one who will criticize you. Your disgrace will become public (375). When your husband comes back and hears of this matter, he is going to say that you should have been willing to accept the offer (580), as this would have been his own wish. You should rather do it quietly, before it becomes public and

you might become an object of contempt for all (585) and they might shame you."
She said: "God forbid that I ever will be disgraced. Here on earth nothing worse
could happen to me (590), if I were observed wallowing in vice and in the greatest
sin, because then the waves of sulphur will torture me in the depths of Hell."

Once this exchange had come to an end (595), the lady lamented: "Oh, dear
Bertram, if you knew of these words, you would immediately return to this coun-
try." This pure lady (600) went to one of her aunts and started talking to her, tell-
ing her that she would complain about this offer to her father. The aunt replied:
"Keep quiet. If you let pass such a rich award (605), neither my heart nor any of
your relatives will ever feel kindness toward you. Even a rich empress can do this
without losing her honor. Once this man will have left you (610), you lock the door
and then you will be just the same as you used to be before."

These words troubled Irmengard deeply, and she returned home immediately
(615), where she went to see her father and her mother. She said: "Good father, and
also my dear mother, listen to this that I need to tell you, I need to share my suf-
fering with you. (620) Help me to carry it loyally." Once her father had learned the
whole matter, he said: "Oh, dear Bertram, if only my daughter Irmengart would be
sound in mind concerning this issue (625) so that she can win this money before
we will lose it! Listen, my dear daughter, drop your soul-searching and comply
with his wish, or you will lose my love. If this money gets lost [because of your
refusal], I will show you my great wrath, and when God will send Bertram back
home, you will truly be blinded." (635)

The lady's misery greatly increased, and tears mightily welled up in her, which
was caused by her chaste modesty. Then she went to Sir Gillam and to her dear
mother-in-law (640) and sat down with them. She lamented her heart's suffering
to them. The father-in-law said: "Daughter, listen, do what they have advised you,
otherwise I will let you feel it (645) with all my might, and your back will receive
a great beating. If you do not gain this money, you will truly have to die once Ber-
tram will have come home." (650)

She lost all joy and she felt deep shame. Once she had listened to these words,
the happiness in her heart was destroyed and totally torn up (655). Her heart was
deeply touched by the strike of sorrow. In her mind she thought: "I must make a
last all-out effort and find out what they really think about this (660) and whether
they will dare to support this in public." She immediately arranged it and called
all her relatives together in a beautiful room (665). They all gave the same advice,
both the women and the men, as they had done before. And I am telling you the
truth, no one deviated from this recommendation. This grieved Irmengard badly
in her heart and almost killed her. They all left her behind in great sorrow, when
the women and men (675) departed without delay.

The lady sat down and cried. She considered her situation from many differ-
ent perspectives and thought how she could overcome this egregious shame and

the sinful burden (680), and how she should go about it to preserve her loyalty toward her dear husband. Many times she spoke: "Have mercy upon me, sweet God, (685) and also Mary, you virginal maid! Allow me to send my lament to you, and so also my great suffering." Then God recognized her great loyalty and inspired her with good advice (690) because He never abandons those who unwaveringly entrust themselves unto Him.

She said to the maid Amelin: "You have truly often given me advice, both privately and in public, (695) that I should acquire this great fortune. Now tell me, do you have the attitude and does it seem all right for you to take one hundred marks and sleep with this man for one night?" (700) She did not need to think long about it and said: "I would accept it for half that much." This soothed her mind, and she encouraged Sir Hogier to send her the money (705). Thereupon she would fulfil his wish. He only had to do it secretly and come to her without being seen when the night would set in. He should wait for her at the gate (710) where the maid Amelin would expect him and would let him in to her lady.

This pleased Sir Hogier very much. He sent the thousand marks to Lady Irmengard, as he had promised her (715). He made sure to arrive right on time. In the meantime Lady Irmengard had dressed the maid in her own clothing and then had herself put on the maid's dress (720). She placed the maid on her own bed, which filled Amelin with great joy. Hardly had the lady arrived at the gate when she noticed that the merchant had arrived (725). She let him in very quietly and welcomed him politely. He believed that everything was happening according to his plan. She asked him to be quiet, (730) with which he complied. He right away slipped more than ten silver coins into her pocket, for which she thanked him much (735) and wished for him that God would strengthen his honor without end and without fail. Then she said: "You do not need to stand here longer: come with me to my lady, (740) to her wonderful bedroom." Sir Hogier followed her quietly since she had asked him to do so repeatedly. All this happened in the dark, and so this man was deceived (745).

Lady Amelin welcomed him kindly. He approached her on the bed. She wore a short silken blouse and a coat trimmed with ermine fur (750). This was all valuable enough. She was only thinly covered and possessed such a shield that she won the victory [over him—here a sexual metaphor]. He did not hesitate for long (755) and quickly tore off her coat. The same happened to the blouse. The woman did not take it without a counter-attack, and hit him with a kiss which almost might have made him lose the victory (760). This aroused his anger because he was a warrior. He tore the shield-cover apart, and aggressively he stormed toward her because he was a monstrous man (765). He desired kisses from her, but the woman knew how to defend herself. So, when he gave her one kiss, he had to let her kiss him twice. This game they played for a long time (770), but the woman won the victory at the end, which he granted her. He succeed in making a great purchase which I also would enjoy when I am lying in bed with a beloved woman (775). Such a purchase does not break an arm or a leg, and one does not fall on any stone which would crack a man's skull.

Sir Hogier was deceived by a fog before his eyes (780), which is true, I am not lying. Sir Hogier and Lady Amelin spent the night with many joys until dawn. I believe that he had never had a better night (785). When the morning star rose, Lady Irmengard walked, which was strange, to her own bedroom [normally she would have spent the night there]. She called: "Get up, sir, you must leave (790), if you want to save your life." He answered: "Lady Amelin, I will do so." Then he turned and said: "My dear lady, give me a little piece of jewelry which will allow me for the rest of my life (795) to think of you." "I have nothing," said the maid. Thereupon he took a small but very sharp knife out of his pocket and cut off a finger from her hand (800). This brought to an end to all her joy. Then he returned home to his country.

When he had come home, he said: "Sir Bertram, I own everything that you have." (805) Bertram replied: "Do not say so, since it is certainly not true." Hogier answered: "Your efforts do not help you; I will not forfeit our wager and have no intention of hesitating (810). I demand everything that is in your possession, both here and at your home." This deeply disturbed Bertram, and sorrow filled his heart. He was greatly frightened, (815) and he thought of his honor: "How did he manage to do this? He must have truly come up with a lie in order to gain control of all my property. My wife is of such a steady nature (820) that she cannot have wavered in her virtue." He said: "Whatever might happen, I will turn to the courts because I have certainly won the wager."

Sir Hogier answered: "That is just fine with me." Both then went to Verdun where the agreement that they had reached was going to be investigated. Sir Hogier was sure to be the winner (830) and said: "Organize a festivity at which we will settle the conflict. There all your relatives shall see who has truly won the victory and who will be delighted about the triumph." (835) Bertram responded: "I would be foolish if I did not follow through with this."

When Lady Irmengard heard of her husband's arrival, she quickly went to him (840) and embraced him joyfully. She welcomed him and said: "My dear lord, your return brings me much happiness. My heart is singing (845) a song of joy because it is so delighted." Her husband thanked her, but sighs made it almost impossible for him to speak, which frightened his wife deeply (850).

The very sad Sir Bertram invited everyone to a big festival. He thought: "Now I had better share all my bread with my relatives, because if I have to hand over all my property to this man (855), then I won't own anything any more. But if good fortune turns toward me and all his property comes into my possession, then it is my full intention to enjoy my generosity." (860)

Many chickens were prepared, and other foods necessary for such a festival. But worries crept into Bertram's heart, which his wife clearly noticed. Modestly she went over to him (865) and said: "My dear lord, tell me what worries you, if you truly love me so much. I will always be loyally at your side." (870) He answered: "My dear lady, my heart is filled with sorrow, but I do not dare to tell you, in your female chastity, and your eyes will see it anyway." (875) She answered: "My heart-beloved husband, keep in mind that I have been obedient to you since childhood and that I have always fulfilled your wishes (880). Therefore you ought to let me know the cause of your worries. My beloved husband, I might easily give you advice which could help you to get rid of your worries (885) and which could turn your situation to the better."

Once he had told her the full truth, she said: "Now be well, your heart should no longer mourn (890). Hogier's cunning cannot help him at all. His property fully belongs to us." The man was very happy about this announcement and joyfully held the festival. Once they had eaten enough (895) and the tables had been removed, Sir Hogier asked them all to be quiet and began to tell them the whole story and why they had been invited. They all turned pale (900) and looked like dead people. Sir Hogier spoke triumphantly: "I can prove everything here." He pulled the maid's finger out of his pocket and said (905), letting everyone see it: "I cut off this finger of hers when I left her bed, and this will be my proof."

All the relatives reprimanded the lady (910) and accused her bitterly. But she said: "I must lament my shame, but you all advised me to do so." But then, with loud laughter, she showed them both her hands, (915) which were unharmed. Sir Hogier was furious because he had lost everything that he had ever acquired. Then Amelin arrived (920) and complained about her suffering. Sir Bertram politely approached his opponent: "Sir Hogier, turn over everything to me." Filled with grief he said: "I'll do so; take, then, everything that is my own (925), but let me be a beggar in your service." Then Bertram married him to Amelin and gave her the hundred marks that she had earned, and so they could marry honorably (930). All the rest he kept for himself.

I have told you this story as a lesson for women and maids, that they should bridle their wild desires by means of chaste habits, which will help them not to lose their good reputation. Ruprecht von Würzburg has composed this tale and has delivered it to you. Now let us pray to God and to the sweet Virgin Mary to free us from worldly dishonor and the terrors of Hell with the power of their merciful hands.

No. 7
Johann of Freiberg: The Little Wheel

The text of this narrative has survived in three manuscripts, two from the early and mid-fourteenth century, the third from the mid-fifteenth century. According to the language used by the author, he seems to have originated from east central Germany—Freiberg is today located between Chemnitz and Dresden just north of the border with the Czech Republic. The narrative might have been composed around 1320 or 1330, but we cannot be certain about this date. Although Johann von Freiberg did not borrow the motif from a known German source, it is often used in Spanish (Juan Ruiz, *Libro de buen amor*, ca. 1330 or 1340), Italian (Sercambi, *Novelliere*, after 1374), and other literatures. A parallel Middle High German story also exists, *Zwei Malern* (today known as *Der Maler von Würzburg*), but the connections between Johann's version and any of these are vague.

EDITION:

Klaus Grubmüller, ed., *Novellistik des Mittelalters*, 618–46.

TEXT

Johann of Freiberg, who is skilled in many aspects, would like to write a little book (5) of extraordinary events. These are true because the person who heard them told and witnessed them assured me of their truth. Now listen, my dear friends (10), to this strange account.

Once there was a burgher in a city who excelled through his virtues. He was honorable and rich (15), and one would not have found anyone at that time comparable to him anywhere in the city. He was praised all over town (20). He lived free of all dishonor. Wherever his name was mentioned, he was well recognized. His wife was beautiful and good (25). Both of them had mild manners and could look forward to an enjoyable old age full of happiness. This citizen had a wonderful house which was frequented by noble guests (30), such as knights and others. They were well received and treated in the best possible manner. At that time this citizen had employed a scribe (35). Let me tell you what kind of person he was: he was well-mannered and honorable. He had set his mind and all his senses on gaining respect (40). Therefore he gladly obeyed women's requests. Still today there are some knights who pursue the same goal by serving ladies for rich rewards (45), but neither for silver nor for gold: instead only for their love. In such fashion this scribe had set his mind. There was also a maid in the citizen's service to whom he was attracted (50). This caused him many worries all day long. Whoever would have caught sight of this maid (55) would have agreed with me that she was, indeed, impeccable. Her hair was blonde and well-kept and very long (60). She had pretty curls and was as beautiful as a doll. She was a slim person and looked lovely altogether from head to toe (65). God had not forgotten anything when He had created her. Her lips were red as rubies, which caused many pangs in the scribe's heart because he was never allowed to kiss them (70). Her cheeks were red like roses.

But when the scribe went to the maid to flirt with her, she welcomed him very unkindly. He wooed her tenderly (75), yet she only said: "You are out of your mind. You talk as if you were mad. It seems to me as if you have fits, which confuses your head. I dislike your talk (80). Restrain your words and leave me, I beg you, alone. I will no longer tolerate it and will report you to my lord." It did not matter in how friendly a fashion he replied (85), she always retorted angrily. When he said 'yes,' she said 'no,' and so they had conflicts. When he said 'black,' she said 'white,' a strategy that she pursued very diligently (90). Whatever he requested from her, she never complied with.

She fought this war with him for a long time until one Sunday when there were many guests from outside in the house, (95) which meant a lot of work. The maid had been awake from the early morning until late in the evening. Finally all the guests had gone to sleep, and the maid was exhausted (100), tired from all that she had to do, so she lay down on a bench. At that moment the scribe came in and noticed that the maid had fallen asleep (105). He sat down on the oven bench, and while she was sleeping, he was awake. The scribe was filled with many strange thoughts which I do not want to discuss here (110). He wetted his finger and rubbed it on a sooty stone. When it was all black, he stood up, took a candle in his hand, (115) and lifted the maid's dress all the way up to her chin, which she did not notice. He observed that her breasts were as round as two apples from paradise (120). Whoever would have been present at that moment would have lost all sadness. I do not want to relate all these pleasures (125) because I am a nobody. For the scribe it seemed as if thousand years were like one day.

She had a beautiful body, shaped as anyone could have imagined (130). She was slim at her waist, and delightful further down to the little garden of roses. Whoever would have journeyed there (135) would have lost all his sadness. Just above the little bush of roses the scribe drew with his right finger a little wheel in the shape as if a little worm (140) had softly crawled there. Now listen how this story continues! Underneath her belly-button, where her skin was white, he diligently drew (145) a circle with black soot, right on her white skin. I really wonder what he might have had in mind since he did not laugh while he was doing this to her. When he was finished with the little wheel, he immediately covered the maid up again with her clothing (150). He kissed her red lips and then turned away, uttering words of lament.

Now let me tell you the following (155): In order to understand what went on in his mind I would have to compare the scribe to a person who would have starved for three days and then would come into a garden and would see much fruit hanging in the trees (160), yet would not dare to pick any. When he left her without having embraced her, that caused him much pain (165) at the bottom of his heart. He went to bed to sleep, yet cried out in misery thinking of the beautiful maid who so adamantly refused to grant him (170) the fulfillment of his wishes. What else should I tell you? He was as filled with desire as a fish who has lost the water and is lying on dry land (175). This was the kind of pain the scribe went through. His heart melted from sorrow and, burdened with many worries, he could hardly wait for the bright day to arrive (180).

When he ran into the maid, he spoke lovingly to her: "May God grant you a pleasant morning!" She answered: "You do not have enough to think about [i.e., Get lost!]). What does it matter to you (185) whether God wants to give me a good morning? If I am going to enjoy a good morning, this would not be due to your good wishes. I can well do without your wish, because it irritates me." (190). He said: "Oh, why do you speak like that now? You talked to me in a very friendly way when I embraced you and I got my wish fulfilled with you. At that time you were very quiet because it was a good wish." (195) She said: "My golly, this is not true. I would rather allow that my skin be flayed and my hair be cut off. You would be truly cursed (200) today and forever if you tried to rob me of my honor with these words."

The scribe spoke: "If you do not want to believe me," said the scribe, (205) "this would chagrin me. I am telling you this without any intention of flattering you, I am serious. I would like to provide you with a sign [evidence] which will force you to admit to yourself that it happened indeed (210). When I lay down with you and it was almost dawn, I drew a little wheel on the front of your belly. I did this before I left (215) because my brain told me to do so, as I have to tell you truly. I have known this even before, that many a woman has such a mind that she does not want to do what one asks her for (220). And before she would do what one might ask her in a friendly way, she would rather say and claim that it had happened in their sleep. Whether you enjoyed it or not (225), this is the truth."

She said: "Really, if this is true, then my hair is golden." He replied: "You may take a look at it, but then you would have admit that I told the truth." (230) She went into the garden and wanted to find out the truth. She stepped behind a tree, put her hand to the hem and pulled up her underskirt (235). Then she discovered a black wheel on the front of her belly. The maid got furious and said: "How did he think of it, or what devil brought him so close to my body? (240) If he made me a woman in my sleep, God has worked a miracle with me. But this cannot happen! (245) How could he have taken my honor in my sleep? I will never believe this." The maid sat on the ground and reflected upon it, turning over many thoughts in her head (250). Then she looked down at the wheel and said: "Scribes know many tricks. Therefore I am willing to believe that he was cunning enough to get down there (255) and take my maidenhood. What childish thoughts and useless doubting, what foolish mind do I have now? How in the world could this have happened (260) that a man would rob me of my virginity in such a way that I would not even notice it?" This way she was heavily burdened in her heart with many thoughts (265). She was filled with pain from the early morning until noon and suffered from great worries. Then she began to think about it anew: "My God, what was wrong with me (270) that he could draw the little wheel on my belly? It seems to me that I was drunk, and so he did to me (275) what he could not, by God, repress. Now I want to go to him and ask and beg him to tell me how it happened to me, poor woman, (280) that I lost my maidenhood."

Now this maid would have sworn that the scribe had made her a woman. Considering this maid, (285) you should notice and observe the meaning of an old proverb which you have heard often: Women have long hair and little reason, that is true (290). The poet Freidank once said: "Women's mind is weak."

The maid thereupon went to the scribe. When she looked at him (295), she said to him, smilingly: "I should be angry with you that you have robbed me of my honor in this way; who gave you permission?" (300) He said: "I did it myself; you can reprimand or hit me, a lot or a little." She replied: "Really, I do not want to hit you or reprimand you (305). But keep it all a secret, I beg you for this favor in the name of your virtue and upon your good manners. Whatever your guilt may be, I still want to make the best of it (310). If I only had enough courage I would like to ask you about something, because my heart is filled with thoughts." (315) He said: "You may ask, I will tell you everything I know." She said: "Then tell me, my dear, and may God grant you a reward for it, how did you gain my love so tacitly (320) that I did not even notice it?" He said quickly: "I lay down with you." "She said: "How? Tell me, then I won't ever lament about it and want to be yours for good." He said: "I must show it to you, I cannot tell you in any other way how we both lay together." (325) She said: "Where, when will this be?" He said: "Be in your bed when the people go to sleep, then no one can chastise us."

The maid could hardly wait (330) until her lord had gone to sleep, and all the servants who lived there. She sat down with the scribe and began to chat with him tenderly, and began to like the scribe (340). Then she said: "It is late, let us go into the bedroom!" [He:] "I would like to go with you there, but I am afraid that we will be noticed. Since the people are still awake (345), they will hear us making noise when we walk through the hallway, which has a high ceiling and is very long, as you know as well." She said: "I will take care of it (350), do not worry about it. I am strong enough to carry you so that no one will notice that we are two." He said: "My dear, are you willing to do that?" (335) The maid answered: "Indeed, yes."

The scribe was not slow; he placed himself on the maid's left shoulder. Watch, he might well sing or speak (360) about his good fortune that such a pretty maid carried him to bed. Would this not be great fortune? I myself would speak of great luck (365) if I would thus be carried to bed.

He said: "You must walk very quietly and move your feet very steadily. Watch out that I do not fall, otherwise people will wake up." (370) She said: "Be quiet, I can handle this; you are lighter than a chicken. By Saint Helena, I could [easily] carry two of you." He said: "My love, is this true?" (375) She answered: "Be assured in every respect that I am not lying to you." She jumped around in the room like a goat (380) with him [on her back]. She even jumped over a tall bench with the scribe on her back, just like a rabbit jumps over a furrow. She performed all these acts to make sure that he would no longer need to question (385) whether she could carry him. She said: "Do you notice how steadily I am standing?" He said: "My love, do not hurt yourself because you have a weak body." She jumped over the threshold like a deer jumps over a creek (390), for almost three yards. She brought him to the bed. The maid was very considerate, grabbed the bolt (395) and locked the door with it. Then she said: "Now rest assured that no one will notice us."

He said: "Take off your dress. Since God has sent us here (400), I will show you very shortly what happened to you the other night." She said: "I have given myself into your power. I want to live as you wish and want to be yours (405). You may now show me whatever you would like to do, and I will not say a word." They took off their clothes and experienced great joy (410). They lay together in full happiness, tightly locked together with their arms embracing each other. Anyone passing by would not have been able to tell (415) who was the woman and who was the man. At the same time both their lips were pressed so closely to each other that one would not have been able to push the petal of a poppy between them (420). He played a tender game with the maid, which the world has known without hatred and without envy, as the world is used to play with love (425).

When she noticed that it was so sweet, the maid said: "I do not want to witness the next day. I would give everything (430) I could acquire in this world so that this game would last until the morning. Even if I could live as long as Elias, or be the ruler in the palace of Rome (435), I would give it up in exchange for my game." He said: "My love, how did you experience it?" [She said:] "No one can give a complete report or fully write about the nature of this love (440). Even if the ocean would be ink, and the sky parchment, and even if the all stars in the sky, both the sun and the moon, grass, sand, and leaves (445), and even if the tiny spot in the sun were scribes, it would be too difficult for all of them to write and report about it completely how wonderful I felt (450). The time seemed to be flying by; I heard singing outside my ears as if little birds were singing and as if a thousand rotes [stringed instruments] were playing. My eyes sparkled with fire (455) as if they saw red roses sprouting in the dew on a green meadow. No one can describe our happiness. A thousand years seem to be like one day (460). At the same time I felt in my mouth honey and sugar powder which flowed down my throat." Again she began to speak (465): "In my mind I imagined that I was floating in the air while I experienced these joys."

When this game had come to an end, she put her hands into the wall (470) and caught two nightingales which sang as loudly as if it was in the month of May. Then the maid said: "When we were about to join (475), there was not even the smallest limb [in my body], believe me that, where there was not a violinist playing the lay of the Elves, which robbed me of my senses (480), so that I could not hear or see anything, so wonderful was my experience. Whoever would beg me even urgently to tell the truth, I would not be able to relate (485) what we both were doing. May God spare you all suffering! Now show it to me a second time, and I want to pay closer attention."

The scribe was not too slow, (490) and granted the maid her wish, that is, four times before the crowing of the rooster, and three times before the rise of dawn. Both the hearts of these lovers lamented that (495) they had to part from each other. He quickly kissed her red lips about a thousand times and said: "May God protect you forever!" Then this worthy man left (500).

Pay attention and notice the message of this tale, you honorable scribes, and strengthen your mind. When you woo the ladies (505), closely study their behavior. Whether maid or woman, whoever among them plays [this game] by force for the first time, will subsequently let it happen again very quickly (510), as you have heard of this maid about whom I told you this story. In her mind she was as hard as a rock (515). When he said "yes," she said "no." At the end he broke her resistance and convinced her to lift him onto her back and carry him to her bed. There all his pain was rewarded (520).

Herewith the tale of the scribe and the maid has come to its end. It is called: The Little Wheel.

No. 8
ANONYMOUS: WOMEN'S CONSTANCY; OR: WRONGFUL SUSPICION PUNISHED

This is one of numerous versions dealing with the same motif, that is, the virtuous and chaste wife and the foolish husband who does not trust her to be chaste, and this against all odds and without any reason. The Middle High German *mære* is most likely based on the Old French *fabliau De la bourgeoise d'Orleans* (fourteenth century), although there the wife commits adultery after all. She successfully deceives her husband by having him badly beaten up, which fully convinces him that he was wrong in his suspicions regarding his wife's adultery; he becomes the *cocu battu et content*. Nevertheless, while the husband is physically abused, the wife enjoys her lover. By contrast, in our case nothing like that happens because the point of criticism rests on the distrustful husband and the most virtuous wife who turns to violence as her last resort in her resolute defense against an attempt to seduce her. Our text has come down to us in one manuscript only, Heidelberg, Universitätsbibliothek, Cpg 341, folios 351r–54v. This is the same miscellany manuscript that also contains Dietrich von der Gletze's *The Belt*.

EDITION

Friedrich Heinrich von der Hagen, *Gesammtabenteuer*, 2: 105–21.

TEXT

Strange things happen often, and one can hear and see them every day. I would like to relate one of these amazing adventures (5) concerning a worthy and rich man. I am going to tell you the story using rhymes as best I can, and will begin as follows:

Once there was a knight in Austria who was free from all faults (10), and who excelled by his wealth and virtues, by the praise that he received and the honor that he enjoyed as foremost among all among his contemporaries, whether they were rich or poor. This noble and virtuous man (15) was married to an adorable woman who possessed purity and a good education. The praise she enjoyed all over the land because of her nobility and kindness was so great that in terms of chastity and constancy (20) not one woman could compare herself to this lady. The knight and his wife led a life filled with loyalty and honor (25).

Then one day an evil thought deranged the husband's mind. It caused damage to the wife, and also was a loss for the husband when he thought to himself (30): "I wonder about my wife and would like to find out whether she might be truly loyal, as she seems to demonstrate through her behavior." Consider how an absurd attitude (35) that lacked all wisdom confused him. The knight had a squire who was loyal and honest. He was of such an origin that he enjoyed the rank of the knightly class (40), as reflected by his own family and his friends. He was called Little Hans. The knight asked him in secret to take it upon himself to woo his own wife (45). As a reward he promised him: "You will always have the privilege of asking me for any favor." The squire: "Sir, please spare me this request since it would be better for your own honor, and do not ask me for this favor (50), considering your courtliness and your public esteem. I think that your request is unwise." Moreover he said: "These are strange things which you, Sir, request from me (55). And by your leave, I would like to reject your extraordinary demand, which your mouth has expressed toward me." Again, however, the knight spoke: "I still say the same thing as before (60). If you do as I am asking you to, you will enjoy great profit from it. But should you refuse to carry out my request, then you would have to renounce all the favors that I have ever granted to you (65). But please understand my request properly. If you ever might manage with adequate strategies that your lady might grant your wish, and if your personality can convince her (70) that she promises you her love, and when it has happened that she pledged herself to you, I want to step in and take your place. This plan will not hurt you at all (75), and it will hurt her very little either. Furthermore, I would like to let you know why I have conceived of this plan. I hit upon this idea because I want to find out (80) to what degree my lady might be steadfast in her loyalty [to me], which is praised far and wide, apart from her beauty that she enjoys. Now, if she proves to be constant and resists your wooing words, which I will teach you (85), I will reward you for this effort."

When the well-educated and cultured squire had understood from his lord that the service (90) would not hurt him if he were to ask his lady for her love in a secretive manner, without incurring any damage and without the danger of losing his honor, he acted as any virtuous servant would do (95). He said: "Sir, I am ready to serve you as you wish because I would like to avoid being accused of having failed in loyalty. That would cause me damage for ever and bring shame upon me without any hope for recovery (100). Lord, by your leave, if you could accept it, I would prefer to be released from this duty. But in order to keep your favor, I am ready to try my wooing [with the lady] in such a manner (105) that God may protect me. This is my deepest request from him, by my loyalty and also by my honor."

With this their exchange came to an end. The courtly and skillful squire (110) was from then on constantly ready to serve his lady, never too tired for it, and this goal he accomplished better from day to day. One day it happened that she was supposed to return from her church service (115), as she had done many times before. The young man did not let this opportunity pass because he was closest to her, either next to her or ahead of her, and complimented her in courtly fashion, as one does still today, as women expect it to happen. All this he undertook right away as best he could. He said: "My lady, grant me your grace (25), because of your virtues, that I won't experience negative consequences from the words that I am going to speak to you, my queen, and which I had hoped to utter for a long time. May this happen by your leave." (130)

The highly virtuous lady answered him in a most courteous manner: "Tell me, my dear Little Hans, what might be the meaning of your words with which you are requesting the privilege to speak freely to me? (35) I have always talked to you as to my other squires. Now freely speak your mind toward me, keeping your honor toward me, and make sure that your words are intelligent." (140)

"Grant me your forgiveness, dear lady, for I have to live in the youthful time of my life. Your beauty and your goodness have so completely overpowered and captured my heart and my mind (145), and this so hard already in my young age, that as a consequence my life has to pass away unless I can find favor with you (150). I need to gain some hope from you, which has been my desire for a long time, looking at you with loyal eyes, keeping my emotions toward you all secretly in my heart."

The lady answered him in the following manner (155), and she was free of all deceptiveness: "You are overly influenced by a habit inclined toward humor and making jokes. Therefore I order you, and this is truly my wish, to keep quiet, spare me your words, and leave me alone with your desire (160), if you want to stay alive."

"Mercy, my lady, you who are so free of blemishes. I have pledged myself and my life totally in your power, and am ready to die (165) for your sake, whatever might please you." Thereupon the pure and lovely lady said: "Your request is foolish, and since you are not willing to renounce your intention, your master will have to hear of this (170); more I am not going to tell you for the next two days."

With these words she went into the house. The squire remembered the agreement with his lord, went to him straightaway (175), and let him know what she had told him. He said: "Sir, your wife is so firm that I do not believe I can achieve anything with my words because she said very angrily (180) that she would complain to you about me." The master answered: "Do not let this concern you. I will deal with it in such a way that she will never mention it to me, neither publicly or privately." (185) Subsequently the squire continued with his wooing as before and again according to his master's request. The wife, who was so constant, politely approached her husband und complained about it in a knowledgeable manner (190), and asked him for the favor to forbid the young man to pursue such erotic desires.

He answered: "Lady, never let me hear a word about it (195). You might thus bring it about that I could lose this servant, which would represent a loss for me. If, however, he did anything else to you, my lady, then let me know it. After all, I have never had (200) such a loyal servant, and it would be grievous to me if you caused him so much trouble that he would lie dead before me. Therefore, my dear wife (205), please dismiss your complaints."

The lady was deeply shocked at his answer; and she had never experienced a more worrisome day in her life; she went through much suffering, because although she had related the squire's words to him, (210) her husband had ordered her to keep quiet about it. This deeply pained her heart. [She prayed:] "Dear God in heaven, help me that no suffering or shame will be brought upon me!" (215)

The courtly and not at all foolish squire asked his lady for her love once again according to his master's request, using eloquent words on many different occasions (220). She said: "Since I have reported it to your master and since he refuses to forbid this [behavior] to you, I am deeply grieved. But I will try, if it is in my power (225), to complain to my friends as soon as the next holiday comes and ask them to make you stop your behavior. If you are not prepared to spare me your [wrong] behavior, you will have to give your life in turn." (230)

He answered: "Lady, I know full well that I will have to die. I am fully prepared to leave everything behind rather than to take back my words [of wooing] which I have spoken to you (235). My life will be pawned for it. But I pray to God that you might change your mind, which I would love to hear."

This conversation took place in secret. But the lady did not give in (240). She thought back and forth how she could protect her honor. Her suffering was determined by two types of sorrow. She thought: "If I were to complain now (245) to my friends and relatives about this man wooing me, they will not be deterred by anything until they will have killed him. But then I will suffer sorrow and pain (250) for the rest of my life [because of my husband]. But if I lose my honor, I will be subject to shame and mockery by society and by God. I do not know what to do." (255) This problem was in her mind both early in the morning and late at night. "Heavenly Queen [Mary]," exclaimed this woman who was so firm in her virtue, "give me advice and arrange it in the best possible way for me (260). I urgently request this from you in the name of your child's honor!" Then the good God planted a cunning thought in her awareness and mind (265) which took away suffering and sorrow from her.

In the meantime the clever squire had quietly returned to the lady in a courtly manner. He wooed her with smart and charming words (270) that came from his heart and his mind, trying the best he managed to do. The lady asked him to sit down and said deceptively: "I have by now realized your constancy (275), since neither my request nor my advice, neither my desperate appeal nor my threats can achieve any change. I have to forgo my honor and must allow you to lie with me (280). I have carefully considered it and decided that it would be acceptable, because otherwise your body and life would be handed over to death. But you are of a noble family (285), so let us no longer postpone it. Now, note well what I am going to tell you: your master wants to go on a journey the next day. Then you may come late at night into my bedroom (290), entering through the little garden where I will let you in myself."

He thanked her for this and was happy. Secretly he then went to his lord and related without delay everything (295) that she had told him. His master answered: "I am telling you, if you are willing to believe me, women have a weak mind, as the poet Freidank tells us (300). All of them would be steadfast only if no one asked them for the favor to grant access to their bodies and their love. This I have now found out."

The lady did not neglect (305) to take all her maids-in-waiting with her to the bedroom, and ordered them to lock the door tightly. An old chambermaid followed her. The lady said: "Young maids, help me (310) to protect my loyalty, and also that I can grow old with my honor intact as it was the case when I got here." They said: "Tell us, lady, how? We are willing and ready." (315) The lady then related to them in all details how the young squire was bent on robbing her of her own honor by asking her for her love, an effort on his part which had already gone on for a year (320). "Now I would like chase him away with a cunning strategy. On Sunday late at night he will come to my bedroom. I will let him in (325), as I informed him. You ladies must stay with me, and when I allow him to enter, then make sure for your life," she said to the [old] chambermaid (330), "that you have ready three strong sticks of wood for the haughty squire, and also three sturdy branches with strong and solid ends with which we will whip his skin (335) and thereby save us from being shamed. She among us who is the strongest must be positioned nearest to him and must catch him by his hair, then throw him down on the floor (340) so hard that the skin on the back and ribs of this monkey will tear. The others must hit him so hard with the sticks and poke him with the branches (345) that he will need water to survive. Let's grease him the cabbage until his damned skin begins to rip open and be tattered. For my sake, do not let up in your beating (350), even if I speak up against it or do something to the contrary. Just hit him very hard."

[In the meantime], the knight was very pleased and said to the squire (355): "I must give you many thanks for this secret operation." Later he went to the lady's bedroom without any hesitation, as his squire had arranged it (360), and knocked carefully at the door. The beautiful and clever woman asked: "Who may this be?" [He:] "Lady, this is Little Hans, your longtime servant and your wooer." (365) [She:] "This seems correct to me; I recognize you from the way you walk and from your voice."

There was a little candle set up somewhere in the back which burned behind a veil and gave only little light (370). [She said:] "Now the time has come to open the door." The door to the bedroom was opened a little, but not too wide, and the man was allowed to enter. The first woman was immediately over him, and she was the boldest and strongest, hitting him with both hands, tearing him badly by the hair, forcing him down on the floor and making him fall against his will (380), crushing his body with loud noise. Three maids, as had been arranged, also threw themselves upon him, and so did the chambermaid. With the strong, hard (385) sticks and the branches they beat him badly, worse actually than any court jester had ever been beaten. The knight ten times regretted (390) his coming there. He called out with a loud voice to the lady: "Mercy, lady, it is me!" But for each yell he received one more hit (395) with the [strong] sticks.

When he had received a thorough beating, worse than ever before in his entire life, such as at tournaments and in battles, he regretted his action more than anything else before (400). Finally she allowed him to swear an oath that, if he wanted to survive, he would be obedient and ready to receive orders, which he also did. He swore upon his manly honor (405) that he would comply with her demands forever and also would avoid doing whatever she might wish him to avoid, as long as he would live.

Thereupon the light that had been kept hidden (410) was turned up again. Only now did the wife recognize that he was her husband. Full of rage, the innocent and good woman (415) asked him about the root of the matter. She inquired what had happened: "Tell me, you evil man, what made you come here tonight in such a secretive manner?" (420) He confessed his great stupidity and said: "The path of misfortune has led me astray, lady. I hope that I can trust your mercy that you will help me recover (425). Have pity on me, I must confess that I acted badly against you; I have been deceived by my stupid imagination."

Then he revealed to her completely how he had asked his servant (430), Little Hans, for a favor. "It was all my fault that he wooed you and asked for your favor." The wife said immediately: "Damn you, distrustful husband! If it were not a dishonor for me, I would let you rot on the bed. Did you believe that I would abandon my constancy and my honor for this squire or for any other man? Nowhere in the world or in Germany do I know a man so attractive or so esteemed, possessing so much wealth, (445) that I would ever be willing to overlook you in favor of him. You have been rightly punished. But as to what you have done to me, I demand better trust (450) than you have demonstrated to me."

The next morning she had a wise man [a medical doctor] come to her, who treated her husband with a good salve that took away his pain (455) and healed his wounds.

Truly, I dare tell you that within half a year he was fully healed. He asked God many times to bestow his reward upon his intelligent wife (460) whom he was determined to trust much more for ever.

On behalf of the wife's honor this short verse narrative (465) was simply and truly called, as I have been told, "Pure Women's Constancy."

No. 9
Heinrich Rafold:
The Hazelnut Mountain

This verse narrative is contained in one manuscript, formerly in Königsberg (today Kaliningrad, Russia), today in Toruń, Poland (Biblioteka Główna, Rps 10/I; folio 19rb-19vb), which dates from ca. 1350 and seems to have been written in Thuringia, as far as the scribe's dialect features indicate. Heinrich Rafold, however, might have been of Bavarian origin, or he might have been related to the dynasty of Nussberg, located near St. Veit in Carinthia (Austria). The poet's formulaic explanation that he was illiterate seems to be a playful approach borrowed from Wolfram von Eschenbach in his *Parzival* (ca. 1205). But possibly Rafold truly was a blacksmith who could not read and write and earned his living through his workshop; after all, his name lacks the traditional 'von' (of) typical (though not exclusively) of persons of aristocratic origin. The narrative was composed sometime in the late thirteenth or early fourteenth century. The motif of love between a Saracen (Arab) and a Christian, leading to an escape of both to the detriment of the husband (here a Christian, normally a Muslim), finds various parallels in medieval German literature, such as in *Salman and Morolf*, Wolfram von Eschenbach's *Willehalm*, and in *Die Heidin*.

EDITION

Friedrich Heinrich von der Hagen, ed., *Gesammtabenteuer*, 1: 441–47.

TEXT

Heinrich Rafold is the poet of this account. He never got any assistance from a schoolmaster and he never learned how to read and write. Since he does not know (5) what has been written down in major works of the past, he cannot find proof for his own tale. His profession is that of a blacksmith [literally: from steel and iron he gains his income]. His heart told him (10) to give an account of what happened once to a knight who was renowned for his honor and virtues. Wherever there was any feuding and fighting, he could easily gain a good reputation (15). He was so famous at his time that he was highly praised everywhere. His own wife, however, did not reward him for that, irrespective of how honorable he was. So here begins the story (20).

We read in a book that there was a king sometime in the past who was powerful and bold. His kingdom was situated near the land of the heathens against whom he often had to fight. (25) Soon it came about that he efficiently built a strong castle, and that is not a joke. This very same king (30) had in his service a high-spirited knight who excelled in loyalty, constancy, and good character. He entrusted the castle to him as his own. It was called *Nussberg* (the Hazelnut Mountain). The knight acquired the same name (35), as I can tell you. He was called the lord of the Hazelnut Mountain because he often carried out heroic feats with manly strength when he fought against the heathens (40).

The war went so well for him that he captured the most worthy man among the heathens, that is, their king; and he also won as prisoners the most noble heathens. He intended to take them all with him (45). When the others realized that their lords were being led away, no one dared to put up any further resistance.

When he had taken the heathen king to his home castle, he thought to himself (50): "Treat him in a princely manner and allow him to walk around freely [upon pledge of honor]." He allowed him to spend his time in the castle without being shackled, (55) and to roam around freely.

Then the knight rode away from his castle and told his king that he had captured the heathen king. This guaranteed him a most honorable welcome (60) by his lord. This news filled everyone with exceeding happiness.

But at home there was no good guard. His wife changed her mind in such a way that it besmirched her honor (65) and robbed her of public esteem. She fell so passionately in love with the heathen king that his love and his pleading made the woman decide to entrust her happiness and her well-being (70) to the heathen man and follow him to his country. The lady badly harmed her honor [through her action], and soon after [she had fallen in love with the king] she went down to the dungeon (75) and liberated the prisoners, the entire heathen company, and did this secretly and without anyone noticing it.

No. 10
ANONYMOUS: THE WARM DONATION

This fifteenth-century verse narrative was traditionally attributed to the mid-fourteenth-century didactic poet Heinrich der Teichner, but modern scholarship has rejected this attribution. The highly popular motif of the housewife who has nothing to give away to a beggar but her own body for sexual gratification because her husband has locked away everything out of sheer miserliness found expression in numerous verse ballads (first printed in 1530 in Nuremberg), and also in a verse narrative from the early fourteenth century, composed sometime around 1320 or 1330 in southern Bohemia. The text was copied down in eight manuscripts, of which one has been lost today, whereas another has survived only as a fragment. The two oldest manuscripts containing this text are housed in Heidelberg (Cpg 341) and Geneva-Cologny (Bibliotheca Bodmeriana, formerly Kalocsa Ms. 1). Folklorists have speculated that the motif of this tale could be traced back to the ancient Indian *Panchatantra*, but there are remarkable differences, and certainly the line of descent eludes us. But the account of the poor suffering wife who substitutes sex for a regular charity donation has enjoyed popularity in songs and tales until the twentieth century. The story's title probably means: a live donation (the woman's body), instead of bread or any other food item, or money.

EDITION

Friedrich Heinrich von der Hagen, ed., *Gesammtabenteuer*, 2: 241–48.

TEXT

[motto:] This is truly a strange story of the clever warm charity donation

Once upon a time there was a miserly man who had the habit of spending very little. He locked everything he owned away from his wife (5), both early in the morning and late at night. He was the most miserly person in the world. He carried the key for all things with him wherever he walked or rode on horseback. He knew exactly how many eggs the chicken had laid for him (10). He counted them every day. His wife could not get even one. His cheeses he had also counted. He did not grant her any control, neither over this nor over that (15). She got hardly anything to eat.

One day he had to go to his mill and she was told to guard the house. Once he had left, a very poor man arrived at her house (20). He implored her in the name of almighty God to give him something [to eat]. The lady lamented bitterly that she had nothing (25), although she would have liked to grant him his wish. She said: "My miserly husband has locked away everything that I own, both meat and bread. Even at the risk of starving to death (30), I would not be allowed access to the food. If you would like to accept my love [instead], I would be happy to share it with you in the name of God."

He answered: "Lady, do not mock me; I am such a poor man (35) that I do not deserve to be ridiculed. If it were true what you are telling me, I would lament it bitterly. [Through my begging] I receive meat and bread (40) enough to feed myself well and do not suffer from hunger."

The lady took him by his hand and led him to her bedroom. Both lay down (45), both the lady and the good man. Look, there he played with her most happily, as is usual among all people [literally: according to the customs in this world]. This way he received his donation and said that he had never (50) received more and greater honor. She said: "What I have given you, I gave you instead of bread. Now take [whatever you want] instead of meat (55), if you like to do so next."

Herewith the good man embraced his lady one more time and took the better donation. Full of eagerness she gave him that (60). He said: "My Lord, Saint Michael, will reward your soul for it! No one has ever given me in my whole life a donation of the kind that she granted me (65). She should be rewarded for it, by the Holy Sepulchre!"

While thanking her with these words he went out of the door. At that moment, when he was already outside, he ran into the husband who heard his blessing and the words of thanks that he uttered (70). The husband ran into the house to find his wife. He said: "Wife, tell me, what did you give to the good man [sic] whom I met when he left the house (75) and who thanked you so exuberantly?"

She answered: "I did not give him anything, because you did not let me have one bit that I might have been able to grant to anyone. I have a soul and know what life means." (80) When he had heard this the husband grabbed a piece of firewood and beat his wife so long that she finally told him the truth. She began to cry and said: "I know one thing for certain (85); the person who wants to enter heaven must first give alms [here on earth]. I have a soul [I am a good Christian] and do not want to live like a heathen woman. Therefore I allowed the beggar to have sex with me [literally: I gave him my love] (90) as endowment for mass service, in the hope that he would later pray for our souls once we are in Purgatory. I did not have anything else available to do penance for your and my sinfulness, and his praying was supposed to serve us both."

When the good man (95) carefully considered her sinful act, it grieved him and made him very unhappy. He cried out loudly and spoke: "Oh dear, why was I ever born? You have lost your honor (100), but it was me who was responsible for it! The sin you have committed you could have easily avoided, but I had locked away from you everything on which you were supposed to live (105) and which you could have given to poor people [as alms]. This is all my fault, at least as much mine as yours. Now, take control of everything I own and that I have ever gained (110), both meat and bread, and give it away to those people who are in need of it. But if you distribute anything else beyond that [such as sex], you will lose your honor."

This way the wife gained control (115) of the power in the house and the key to everything, and from then on she enjoyed a happy life. Since that time she could grant alms as much as it pleased her.

However, there is one thing that puzzles me, and I ask you to think about it (120). Would a woman nowadays do the same thing [as this wife had done] if she had nothing else to hand out? I am telling you very specifically, and you can trust me: a woman would give even more alms who would give them out of love (125) for almighty God in Heaven.

Herewith our *mære* has come to an end. Women could always live without suffering from grief if they give such a donation.

No. 11
ANONYMOUS:
THE MONK WITH THE LITTLE GOOSE

This anonymous verse narrative has come down to us in six of the major manuscript collections holding the largest corpus of late medieval German *mæren*, dating from the first quarter of the fourteenth century and extending to the middle of the fifteenth century. The anonymous author might have composed it sometime in the second half of the thirteenth century, although the earliest written copy dates from ca. 1320/1230. According to the linguistic features, the author originated from the Alemannic region in southwestern Germany. The didactic intention, nicely enveloped in a humorous tale, appealed to many sermon writers and didactic poets. Whereas the unknown original source was certainly oriented toward moral and ethical teaching, the present text depends heavily on the interest in the comic and entertainment aspect.

EDITION

Rolf Max Kully and Heinz Rupp, eds., *Der münch mit dem genßlein*, 72–81.

TEXT

I have heard that once there was a rich and well-constructed monastery, just as a monastery was supposed to be built. [It was so rich] that its inn and hospital (5) did not even follow the strict meal plan [stipulated for the monks]. Whenever a traveler arrived there on foot or on horseback, he could get a meal ready-made. Everyone received (10) whatever food he desired, a practice which really should be followed by all monasteries today.

Whoever was in charge of the gate was instructed upon the penalty of death (15) never to admit any woman. Those who held that position made sure to protect the lifestyle of the convent strictly, which was their privilege (20). I was also told that their convent was so hidden away that neither the monks nor their servants hardly ever saw anyone else. Moreover, I was also told (25) that the convent had many members who never left the enclosure.

Once there was a young man who had spent all his life in the convent (30) since his childhood. For that reason he knew nothing about customs in the world, so he had no idea of horses, carts, or sleds (35) which people use for transportation. Then it happened that the abbot wanted to travel on business for his convent. The young man begged him (40) to take him along into the world so that he would learn about it. The abbot granted him his wish without hesitation. Since he knew of his simple-mindedness (45) he took him along. The servants did not stay behind, and rode off with their master. Their horses rode smoothly. When they got to the open area (50) they saw many different kinds of animals. The monk did not give the abbot any rest, and asked him immediately what the name of every animal was. The abbot told him all the names right away (55), whether they were cows, oxen, sheep, rams, asses, or swine, and identified each one of them.

Soon they reached (60) a farm which was their first destination, and where they wanted to stay for the night. When the farmer saw them he ran toward them and shouted: "Be welcome, my lord (65), and all of them who accompany you." When the [farm hands] had received the horses, the abbot and the monk went to an open fire in their room as the first thing (70). The servants quickly took off their shoes and their coats.

Now the farmer had a wife and a daughter, whose body was so shaped as to please everyone (75). She was about twenty years of age. The daughter also came into the room and greeted the lord in friendly fashion. The abbot asked her to sit down, so she did not leave again (80), but instead she took a seat. The young monk asked the abbot to let him know the name of this creature. The abbot answered without delay (85): "These are called geese." The monk replied: "My gosh, then geese are beautiful! How come we do not have geese [in the convent]? They might do really well there." Both the innkeeper's wife and her daughter laughed heartily at this statement. They were amazed at the attractiveness of this young man (95), even if he did not know how women were called. They secretly asked the abbot whether the monk was sane. The abbot told them (100) the same thing that I have told you before, how the young man had gotten to the convent and had grown up there.

When the farmer's daughter learned of this amazing account (105), she thought to herself right away: "This is an attractive man: I would like to see what he can do. I will test tonight whether his body knows how to use (110) women in bed." She liked the monk very much, but she did not tell anyone what she had thought about him (115).

Then it had gotten so late that the men wanted to go to bed. The farmer made sure that they got beds according to their customs. His daughter came along (120) and arranged the beds so that the young man was located far away from the abbot, so that the lord would have his peace (125). This was all her strategy. Once the visitors had been put to their rest, the farmer ordered all his servants to go to sleep as well and to allow the lords to enjoy their peace (130).

The young man could not fall asleep because he was thinking about how everything was called, as he had been told during the day. The virgin also lay in her bed without sleeping and thought about many things, wondering how she could realize the plan that she had developed before.

When all the people were asleep everywhere, she got up without making any noise (140) and tiptoed across the room to his bed. When the monk noticed her he said: "Who might this be?" [She said:] "It is me, the young goose, and I have suffered greatly from the cold (145). My dear lord, I would like to beg you to allow me to slip into your bed. You would help me avoid freezing to death, because it is cold." The monk was so naive (150) that he let her come under the blanket. He had no idea what was going to happen as a consequence of her joining him in his bed. The young man did not know what to do with her (155), and was unfamiliar with what is called the 'bed game.' However, she knew a little more about it, and skillfully she managed to instruct him quickly in how to play this game (160).

The monk made very good use of the goose, because he thought that he had never enjoyed anything better than this game. They kept busy until the early morning (165). Then she got up and said: "You must not say anything to anyone abouy what has happened tonight. If the abbot finds out about it, he will quickly (170) put us both to death." Very seriously she forbade him to reveal anything to anyone. He promised her to do so, and she left him, returning secretly to her room (175). She was delighted that she could get back without anyone noticing her.

Soon afterwards the day broke (180), and the abbot rose from his bed. The monk was mightily pleased. They got up and finished their business which had been the reason for their trip (185). Once they were done with it, they did not want to tarry much longer and desired to return home. When they had come home, the other monks took the young man aside (190) and asked him immediately how he liked the world outside the convent. He began to tell them how many things he had seen in the world (195) which he had not known before. They were bemused by his words, but he was smart enough not to tell anyone that at night during the journey (200) the goose had come to him, though it had not been offered him for purchase. He kept it a secret, just as she had ordered him, and did not let anyone know about it.

One day, shortly before the great holidays (205) that fall in winter and are called Christmas, the abbot sent for his steward and cook. He said to them: "A special week is approaching (210) during which we will have to sing and read a great deal. Take good care to provide us with sufficient nourishment, because when someone works hard, he deserves to be cared for even more." (215) The two servants promised to be diligent. At that moment the young monk was present as well and said: "Since you are prepared to provide us with good meals, you should not forget (220), my dear lord, to let each man have a little goose. Then everyone here will have the greatest joy they can ever have here on earth and beyond." (225) The abbot was very suspicious of his words and told him to be quiet. He complied. But then he said once again: "Geese are the best enjoyment, better than all others (230) that people have ever known."

The abbot said to the young man: "Brother, do not say any more! Alas, what has happened to your senses and your mind? (235) You should know for yourself that we do not eat meat. I will make sure that you will have to do penance for this!" Then he ordered him to leave (240). The monk did not dare to stay, but he said again: "Whatever will be my punishment, I know that geese are, for those who can have them, very good and pleasing." Thereupon he was chased out of the room (245), while the other servants stayed behind and deliberated their meal plan. Then they discussed their program of songs and the readings, and who should be leading the liturgy (250). When everything had been planned, the abbot signaled to the young man once again and took him away from the people to a quiet location (255). He urged him strongly to reveal to him why he had uttered those words requesting the geese. The young man did not hesitate (260) and confessed to him, since he had appealed to him so dearly, how on their journey the young goose had come to him during the night, and how he had let her come under the blanket, (265) and what he did with her.

When the abbot had learned all this, he sadly spoke the following words: "Believe me, this was a woman. Your foolish body (270) has lain with a woman. I should have taken better care of you; then I would have acted more properly." He ordered the young man to kneel down (275) and to do penance, with which he complied.

I think he [the abbot] did wrong to him because the sin that the young man committed was really the abbot's fault (280). If he had told him the truth without mocking him, he would have protected himself well. Lying and mocking are rarely any good. They are sins without any honor (285). What shall I tell you further, beyond what I have already told you? I believe and am convinced that there are monks here in this world, one, two, or maybe three, (290) who all have more intimate experience with women [than the young monk]. If they provoke their lord's wrath, they ought to do penance, that is my advice.

Now my story comes to its end. It is called (295) "The Monk with the Little Goose." It deals with the young monk who made love with the little goose and yet did not realize that he had committed a sin. Still he did his penance (300) according to his abbot's command. He paid for his sin without being guilty of a sin. This is enough said about the clever little goose.

No. 12
Anonymous: The Priest with the Rope

This narrative has come down to us in three rather distinct versions, A (Ak and An), and C. Here the version Ak serves as the basis for our translation. Version Ak is contained in a manuscript today housed in the Badische Landesbibliothek Karlsruhe, cod. Karlsruhe 408 (formerly Durlacher Hs. 481), folios 107ra–111ra, dated ca. 1430. The author is unknown, but he seems to have originated from Schwäbisch-Hall. A parallel version, housed in the Germanisches Nationalmuseum, Nuremberg, cod. 5339a, folios 164r–176v, reveals very distinct differences and contains only partially the same verses. Whereas the narrative in Ak concludes without any moral evaluation, the Nuremberg version warns against untrustworthy advice from women. A third version, C, also in the Germanisches Nationalmuseum, 2⁰ Hs. Merkel 966, ends with a harsh condemnation of the female protagonist. The narrative motif finds many parallels in late medieval literature, highlighting, if viewed negatively, women's cunning tendency to cheat on their husbands, and, if viewed positively, women's intelligence and resourcefulness in pursuing their individual erotic happiness, ridiculing their foolish husbands.

EDITION

Rolf Max Kully and Heinz Rupp, eds., *Der münch mit dem genßlein*, 140–55.

TEXT

It is a waste of effort when you try to tell a story amidst a lot of noise. The storyteller realizes that no one is listening to him, and he feels as if he were a stalker in the moor. Would you, my lord, however, like to listen (5), and hear an instructive tale which I have composed? I have created it based on my own imagination. Now understand: There was a man in a village (10) who was married to a beautiful woman. She was lovely to look at. Both of them were young and rich. The woman was really pretty. There was a priest in the village (15) who knew well how to sing and to read. Many times he went to the woman's house, and she came out of the door and greeted him in friendly fashion with polite words (20). [He said:] "Lady, if you do not mind, I would like to ask you for a favor. If you react with anger, I will lose my life." She said: "My lord, what do you mean? (25) Let me know the meaning of your words. I might easily fulfill your wishes." He said: "Let me lie down with you! I will reward you (30) with my body and my money." [She answered]: "I live under such protection that even if I were such a loose woman and would like to do it, it won't be possible (35). I am married to a young man who stays at home both day and night. For this reason it won't be possible." He said: "This does not worry me; instead, if you are willing, it will happen (40). If you are truly interested in me, he cannot guard you well enough. Wherever two people are in love with each other, they steal their love like a thief." She replied: "If my husband were to find out our love affair (45), it would turn into a bad game. My husband has many friends. However, I know you so well that I do not dare to reject you (50). If I were bold enough to let you go filled with wrath, you might easily place a church ban on me. Thinking about the steps into the church, I would be scared of you both." [He:] "Then do what I would like you to do." (55) [She:] "Well, then you had better come tonight in the early stage of the night through the shed for the sheep. Recently, we have had an opening made (60) near the chimney on the threshing floor so that we might be able to watch over everything we possess in this house. My lord, pay attention to my advice: I will give my husband so much to drink (65) that he will fall into his bed due to his sleepiness. This will give us the right opportunity. You no longer have to beg for my love. I will attach a rope (70) to my toe and to the window. When you arrive here, take the rope into your hand and pull it a little to find out whether I am asleep (75). I will immediately understand the meaning of it and will quietly sneak out of the room. We will both fulfill our desire. My husband will never find out about it. You will have a great time with me (80) and get all your wishes fulfilled until you will be exhausted. My husband will sleep all the time, not noticing my return, which will be our great profit." The priest said: "This would be really good." (85) [She:] "Go home and follow my advice." He returned home and was happy. The lady ordered a sumptuous meal to be prepared for their evening dinner when they ate and drank a lot (90). The lady often clinked glasses with him and drank and encouraged her husband to drink as well, so much that he could no longer speak clearly. The husband did not understand what was happening (95). She [finally] said: "Let us go to sleep." Her husband was immediately ready to do so, happily lay down, and fell asleep right away. When the lady observed this (100), she picked up the rope as she had said to the priest. Then she lay in the bed and stayed awake. Her heart desired, when the priest would come, (105) to embrace him lovingly.

The priest was afraid to arrive too early. The lady fell into a sweet sleep. She had attached the rope to her foot (110) and hid it under the blanket. But see, then the knight of a husband, who had been lying next to her, woke up. He got up as he was wont to do and intended to relieve himself (115). Now listen and pay attention: he came across the rope which he grasped with both hands. Anger and wrath swelled up in him. He followed the rope in both directions (120), until he found the two ends. He immediately thought to himself: "What has the wife planned to do with it? Did she perhaps intend to catch mice or birds of prey? (125) It might well be that she is wooing a squire or a nobleman." Then he lay down again and said to himself: "My Lord, help me." He put on some clothing (130), took off the rope from her foot and attached it to his toe. The woman slept through it all.

The priest came running to the house and got to the point where the other end of the rope was (135). Now listen to what he did: quietly he pulled the rope. The smart husband got up and tiptoed to the door. He opened it and went outside (140). The priest welcomed him tenderly, but I think that he did not get his wish fulfilled because his plan utterly failed. The husband yelled: "Get up, wife, and light the fire, my dear! (145) I have caught a thief, indeed. Tomorrow he will have to die by hanging." These words shocked the wife. Immediately she got up (150) and quickly ran to the fire. She had no reason to laugh. She pushed the coals apart [to keep it from lighting up]. The husband struggled with the priest, pushing him against a chair (155), and made as much noise as if he were in a mill. The farmer was fierce and fumed, but the priest was extraordinarily strong. Both defended themselves well and held each other by the throat (160). Both suffered pain. The husband called out to his wife: "Will you make a light for me?" She answered: "You must do it [I cannot get it going]. If you do not believe me, let me hold the thief and you can try yourself to get a fire going, which, as I guess, will not be possible for you." He: "Come here and hold him tightly! He will have to hang from a branch (170) and swing from the gallows. That's what I will grant him tomorrow." The husband looked for flames and straw, which pleased the priest mightily. When the husband released him from his hands (175), the wife pushed the priest into the shed through a hole [in the wall]. This was his rescue, and he quickly ran home. The wife grabbed her donkey (180) by the neck behind the ears and said: "Look at this fool [of a husband]! What kind of a thief did he give me? He does not mind leading a shameful life!"

When the light was lit, (185) the husband called to his wife: "Give me back the thief!" [She:] "Now see, this is just wonderful. Today he carried our wood. Is this the reason why you beat him so badly? (190) You are dumber than a calf. I believe that you are deceived by a nightmare. Fortunately for us, no one has seen it. Bless yourself, how was it possible that no one noticed it?" (195).

He grabbed his wife by the hair and threw her down on the floor, yelling: "Give me back the thief!" Then he dragged her to the door, threw her out, (200) and let her lie there. Then he went back to sleep. The wife sat down on a bench. Her many tears had soiled her clothing (205). An old woman came by at that moment, carrying her distaff. She said: "I wonder who is crying here, indeed, I would like to know it." The wife said: "Neighbor, let me share my suffering with you (210), since my husband has beaten me." The other: "Oh, this may be lamented to God! What did you do to him? What did this evil man blame you for? May he live in shame!" (205) She answered: "I will give you a vessel full of good flour, if you stay here in my place, and also a piece of bacon, two inches thick. Just sit down here on the bench (220) and cry loudly as if you were me, which will allow me to share my laments with my mother in the village." The old lady said: "What you plan to do is good!"

The old woman sat down on the bench (225) and said: "Well, I can cry and sob better than you, if you are willing to give me these things." The wife responded: "I will surely do so." She ran off to the priest (230), with whom she enjoyed a wonderful time. They played many love games. In the meantime, the old woman sat there and sobbed, as she had been asked to do.

But the farmer did not sleep (235). He yelled to the woman: "Be quiet, stop crying! Come in and close the door. Control yourself better!" She: "You will suffer shame before I'll do it!" (240). He: "You intend to continue with your crazy behavior?" She: "Before I'll stop, you will have to burn first and turn into a wild dog!" He came immediately, rushing out of the house. The old woman could not defend herself (245). He pulled her off the bench by her hair and kicked her and stomped on her as if he had been asked to do so, though she hardly survived it. He cut off her braids (250) and said: "God will condemn you to death tomorrow. These braids I will show your friends and my friends tomorrow." Then he went into the house and locked the door.

The wife, meanwhile, (255) said to the priest: "Dawn is coming, I cannot stay any longer." He said: "Lady, I still have to write you a letter." The lady was easy to persuade because she thought that it would be good for her (260). She stayed there until the priest had written three letters. Then she said: "I want to go!" He said: "So be it." The priest then allowed her to depart. She returned to the old woman (265) who was still lying on the bench. She said: "What are you doing? It is daylight." She replied: "What could I do? Woe is me, and ever woe! I have to complain about your husband (270) and about the terrible time [tonight]. He had almost killed me, which I must lament to God! I would have hardly survived it. He cut off my braids (275) and threatened me that he would show them to your friends and to his own friends." The lady: "Well, then my plan is going well and will turn into a great game for me (280). I will give you twice as much of what I had promised you before. I will certainly promise you that. And I will give you two chunks of cheese."

The old woman crawled home again (285), whereas the young woman sneaked into the house and woke up all the farmhands and maids. She told them: "By God, what a pity that you did not witness it in your sleep and did not see (290) what happened to our lord! He pulled our donkey back and forth, being deceived by a nightmare, which has been his problem for four years now." The farmer then got out of his bed (295) and said to the maids and farmhands: "Today I want to have festivities. Work hard today and prepare it well so that I can gain honor (300) from the people who will be my guests. The costs won't matter to me. Prepare the food: I want to invite everyone."

His wife said: "Let's do it." She told them to kill many chickens (305) and said: "My dear husband, let me know, as your virtues command you to do, what you know about the events that happened at night. May God chase away the evil spirit that has haunted you." (310) Her husband turned away from her and left the city. He invited all their friends, such as her father and mother, her sister and her brother (315), and four of her friends. They agreed to come right away. He himself went to the specific point and asked his own father to join him, and also his mother and his sister (320), his brother and a cousin as well. Moreover, he asked many of his friends to come there. They all said: "We will happily meet you there, and do not want to tarry." (325)

Then she said to her husband: "It is time to eat." All of his friends joined him, and the meal was pleasantly prepared (330). They placed the tablecloths, washed their hands in water, and sat down. They drank and ate. The host was just too generous, when he served them food (335) of many different kinds. It would have been too much even during the Shrovetide season.

But let me shorten the tale: the host sat down with them all (340). He ate little because he was so angry and because he thought how he could tell everyone shocking news [about his wife] concerning what had happened to him at night with his wife and the rope (345). The wife, whom the husband had [allegedly] beaten up, walked around to every table. She had bound her hair in a bundle and wrapped it in a scarf. The husband thought about it (350): "I have the braids with me. It won't matter how arrogant you are, you will have to pay for your evil deed. Nothing will avail me in this case (355) unless I reveal everything to my friends."

She [, on the other hand], whispered to them all: "Whether you like it or not, my husband has lost his mind, and this has been the case already for four years (360). Unfortunately, he is suffering from the evil spirit [the devil] and might be frothing at the mouth for days when he begins to scream. When he will begin to beat me in front of all of you (365), come forward and hold him tight with your hands until I grant him repentance. Now I know how to do that."

Then the farmer said (370): "Since you have come here, let me tell you all everything." He began immediately to complain about the rope, what he did with it (375), and how he had captured the evil thief. Moreover, he told them how she had let him get away again. "Because of these evil things, I ask you to divorce us two. People will reprimand you (380) when they will hear of all this." She replied: "He is telling you a lie. I am sick of his foolishness. In as much as no one has ever criticized him, I have kept quiet about it for four years (385) and suffered under it because of my womanly honor."

The husband spoke up in front of them all: "She is not telling you the truth. I cut off her braids (390) in the night." She said: "Show them to us!" Then he put his hands into his boots and pulled out long braids. She said: "Now you can see (395) that he is not telling the truth and [unjustly] blames me for lying. These [braids] are from a witch, whereas I have not lost mine." She pulled out two blond braids (400) [from her headgear] and let them hang down. He was badly chagrined that she spoke thus in front of them all. He did not remain sitting any longer, and, abandoning all his good manners, (405) he gave her a hard blow. The woman quickly pulled him toward her [and yelled]: "By God, why do you stay in your seats? Get up and help me!" Quickly they came rushing forward (410) and held him until she had tied him up in a big flour trough. Because of his fury he looked like a goat. Whenever he swore that he had not lost his mind, no one believed a word (415). Then he swore most strongly by the Holy Ghost, the Father, and the Son [but to no avail]. She said: "What shall we do? Let us take this miserable scoundrel (420) to my lord Cyriac [martyr, patron saint in emergencies]. I am certain that he will help him get better." They lifted up the fool and carried him in a container (425). They sang *Kyrieleison* loudly and took him to the church that was more than a mile away. That church was dedicated to the merciful Saint Cyriac (430). They put down the container. The wife gave his coat to the church as an offering. Then she cut his hair and carried it, together with the offering, [to the altar] (435). All the friends happily approached the altar [to pray]. The very same priest who had fought with the farmer arrived on his horse. He stepped up to the altar (440). They all participated in the mass and prayed loudly to the saint, begging him to have mercy on the farmer whom they had brought here. The priest said: "He will be helped." (445)

After the mass had been completed, he came to the farmer and prayed. The farmer said: "Sir, stop your praying. I was in full command of my senses in the night, so help me, my lord!" (450) [The priest:] "Be quiet; do not yell in front of all these people, you are still out of your mind!" Then he took the liturgical vessel (455) and swung it over his head. [The farmer]: "Do you want to drown me? The water is dripping into my mouth." Again he swore that he had a sane mind (460). But no one believed him at all. The wife said with a loud voice: "Listen, all you people! I know of a strategy to achieve repentance, which will remove his craziness." (465) She took a light and incense and burnt with it nine holes into the fool's head, in the back, and in the front of his hair.

"Oh!" he screamed out loud (470): "Why are you burning my head? Let me swear to you all, on the honor of my rank as a farmer, I have regained my right mind!" Thereupon they all praised God. She [the wife] said: "Your craziness is gone," (475) and took off his fetters. She led him to the altar, where she found a crucifix and a psalter, which she attached to him. This allowed him to regain his sanity (480). He said: "Holy Cyriac, who has bestowed so much grace upon me, and our beloved God, spare me this suffering from now on forever, (485) for the sake of both our honor! From now on I will always trust my wife. She has suffered because of me." She said: "Yes, upon my oath (490), I had to think of many strategies to restore your sane mind."

They brought him home to his farm as if he were a bishop. Whenever he observed anything since then (495), he never said anything to anyone. [He thought:] "If I let anyone know about it, my wife, whom I observe, will say that I, the fool, am sinning again." (500) He let his head hang down and feared his wife a great deal since then. He was afraid that the evil woman might hurt him again; he feared the shame (505), and worried that she might burn his head.

More I cannot tell you. May God help us! Herewith the story of the rope, (510) which tells about how the lady and the priest mistreated the poor man, comes to its close.

No. 13
"Konrad von Würzburg":
The False Confession

Although the narrative speaker at the end of this tale identifies himself as Konrad von Würzburg (fl. ca. 1260–ca. 1300), this seems to have been a literary ploy and is not taken seriously by modern scholarship on the basis of the manuscript tradition, the style, and the topic of this *mære*. In all likelihood the actual poet resorted to the pseudonym, or *plume de lettre*, of Konrad von Würzburg because this name guaranteed literary esteem and fame. Considering the context, content, language, and the manuscript tradition, this "Konrad" might have lived around 1400, at a time when many of these erotic tales were composed and subsequently recorded on parchment. The text has survived in only one manuscript, Munich, Staatsbibliothek, cgm 714, written between 1455 and 1458, probably in Nuremberg, but Heinrich Kaufringer (version B) and Hans Schneeberger (version C) composed very similar tales that differ only in the degree to which difficulties have to be overcome until the lady has attracted the young man's attention and until he has found a way to come to her bedroom.

EDITION

Klaus Grubmüller, ed., *Novellistik des Mittelalters*, 524–42.

TEXT

Once I heard an amazing story, of which a man who was on a pilgrimage gave me a truthful account about where and when it happened. I am going to tell it to you just as he told it to me (5). I worked hard for four days, giving it my full attention until I had rendered it in verse. If someone might be able to compose it better, I would be happy if he were to do it, (10) and I would joyfully laugh with him about these funny things. Many compose very serious texts, and I would recommend them to present something entertaining as well from time to time (15) because it would alleviate worries. I cannot tell you the story in any better way.

This man [who told me of the adventure] lived in Rome. But what might have been his name, except for being a Roman? (20) He possessed much intelligence, and on top of all of his worldly fortunes he had the pleasure in his life to be married to a completely beautiful woman. She strove, day and night, (25) for loyal love and constancy toward her husband. Everything her heart desired her husband granted her. He was always ready to get rich and fine clothing for her, (30) which meant that she cost her husband a lot of money, as I have heard. He believed that she was free of all [character] blemishes.

There was a street passing by their house (35) which was used by most people. A young nobleman from the city fell passionately in love with her and often went up and down the street. This young man was attractive and intelligent, (40) and was richly dressed in clothes tailored in the French style. Many of his serving-men accompanied him, according to the courtly custom, (45) who were of assistance to him all the time. This young man was twenty-four years old. His beard had begun to grow only recently. He had not yet cut his long hair (50). The young man descended from a noble family, to judge by his friends and wealth. He had a joyous attitude.

Now this beautiful Roman woman was, in her heart, mind, and all her senses, passionately in love with this young man (55), and burned with desire for him.

One day her husband went on a journey. This did not cause her any grief, and she [actually] felt exceedingly happy about it (60). She quickly came up with a plan. This really smart woman went to a Franciscan friar and said certain things to him in a false confession. The good monk listened (65) and thought how to give her advice. She said: "Lord, a young gentleman has sent me a beautiful golden ring—what a young, stupid, foolish young man—and requests my love (70). But I am so loyal and constant in my feelings, even if he had more than three thousand barrels of gold, I would not take it, my dear trusted father [orig. 'brother'] (75), since I would not want to harm my honor so shamefully, which would make my friends feel embarrassed." Then she revealed to him the name of the young gentleman so that he could recognize him (80). When she had identified him, she produced [from her bosom] a ring which was made in masterly fashion and artistically, embellished with a gemstone set into it. She said: "Dear father, please let me ask you (85) to bring back this ring to the miserable young man and order him, in the name of his good education, that he should, if he is descended of a noble family, avoid the street (90) for a while until my husband comes home again. I am afraid that people will form opinions about these events more than at normal times. My house is almost devoid (95) of all servants. People are so quick in developing ideas, both here and there, I am afraid that I will be the topic of much rumor."

The good and simple monk took the ring, (100) not thinking through all the implications, and sought out the young man where he found him alone, offering advice with the power of his rhetoric. He took him by his hand (105) and repeated all the words he had heard from the woman. He said: "Let your efforts go, because it might cause great damage, perhaps murder or manslaughter (110). The lady enjoys the support of her friends, just as you do, according to my knowledge. God Himself says that one should resist evil intentions. Let such things disappear from your heart: (115) that is my advice."

The young man answered: "Lord, whom do you have in mind with this and whom do you suspect of wrongdoing? Perhaps you are taking the wrong route here (120). Honestly, it is not me." The monk responded: "Why do you deny it? I will give you the proof of it now that she sent against you. You had put it into her hand before." (125)

The young man turned pale in his face. He stood there for a while and thought about this and that until he hit upon the truth. He thought, someone had laid a snare to catch him in love and in an affair (130). He concentrated very hard on it and thought: "You should go for this adventure because of this beautiful and attractive lady. She who has sent you the gift has appealed to you to enter into an affair." (135)

He said: "Lord, I must admit, if you had not done something, perhaps I might have committed a great foolishness. Since the lady has told you the entire beginning of the story (140), I will tell you what she gave me as a gift: a beautiful and flawless ring made out of gold and gems, which is very valuable. This stone makes bleeding stop (145) and also helps fight against depression. Her gift, however, does not mean a thing to me and will not be of any value to me ever, since she does not desire real love."

The monk answered: "It pleases me (150) that you have revealed your intentions so knowledgeably. Because of you I can count on gaining holiness because you desire to be God's child. Whoever will be one of my fellow brothers (155), they will have to pray for you, with great devotion, for a good outcome." He gave his hand to the young man (160) and said: "I do not want to tarry any longer since I have the ring [back from you]. Otherwise I would never find a moment of rest."

In the meantime the lovely lady (165) had entered her palace and sat on a bench as if she were a queen. Her elegant clothes were long and well tailored (170). When she noticed the monk approaching the building and rushing toward it, and that, as a result of his great effort, his eyes were swollen red (175) and sweat was on his forehead and cheeks because of his loyal service, the lady got up politely and welcomed him (180).

He said: "I have suffered much pain." She: "What good news are you carrying with you?" He said: "I have fulfilled your wish according to your heart's desire. [But] why did you not tell me anything about the ring?" (185) She said: "Indeed, it used to be mine. I gave it to him because I thought that I also should send him a gift in return, otherwise he would have diminished my honor (190). I know that for sure. It happened only a short time ago that he passed by on my street and through the doorway tossed a belt and a purse directly into my lap (195). I was greatly surprised. The ring was in the purse, along with a letter. I thought: 'What might it say?' It did not speak of anything other than love. This made me really angry in my mind (200). I took it to the fire and immediately threw it into the flames. Honestly, it is burned. This soothed my anger (205). In the letter he explicitly swore that, if he kept his health and his strength, he would try this very night to climb up my wall. I have also found this written in the letter (210). He also wrote that the back of the house had a dilapidated wall in which one board was rotten. If he were to move it just by a hair, it would fall out. This is true. This removal [of the board] (215) will make me to the object of mockery and public rumors among my neighbors. For this reason I will have to be on guard and stay awake tonight."

Immediately the good monk said (220): "You can sleep free of all worries until tomorrow morning. On my honor, he will not do anything to you. Let me know if anything happens to you."

She asked the monk to sit down, (225) and modestly walked away. When she was out of his sight, she jumped up and down. She said to her maids: "If you care to stay in my service (230), I'll be able to manage to gain the dear fruit, my most beloved young nobleman, who will lie in my arms tonight." She went away and opened her treasure chest, from which she took a belt and a purse (235), as I have been told. The belt was of a beautiful intense color, as I am going to tell you next. It was red, green, white, and yellow; it was long and thin (240). It was the rope of great love. The lady did not wind the belt up. Instead she carried it unwound to the good monk and asked him to hide it underneath his garb (245).

He said: "Truly, I am telling you, I will not rest until I will have found him [the young man] again. I pledge this to you: I will instill remorse in him (250) and make him think of God and pay little attention to you."

Her actions then brought it about that this good, simple man, this monk, turned into a matchmaker, a role to which he would not have agreed otherwise (255), if he had known better how to understand women's nature.

The monk immediately went to the location where he found this young man, this outrageous person. He told him the woman's intentions (260), everything down to the last detail, and then gave him the belt. He asked him about the letter which was a torture for his soul: "Who has written the letter for you (265), which was in the purse, which is still attached to the belt? Who taught you this skill? I am really surprised." Then he asked him further on (270) regarding the board and the wall and informed him about all aspects that the lady had mentioned.

Thereupon the young man responded: "Lord, I really regret it (275) that this great foolishness ever came upon my heart (275). After all, she is married to a nobleman who is handsome and wealthy, and no one would have any right (280) to criticize him for anything. May God give you a reward because you have given me a lesson! My heart was confused, which will never happen again, by God (285). On my honor, I will not bother her any more, irrespective of how wealthy and beautiful she might be. I will never approach her again."

The monk quickly returned to his cell (290) in which he sang and read what was soothing for his soul.

The young man was filled with great desire for the lady because his heart was embraced by her love (295) and had even entered it. When the day came to its end and night was near, he went, after he had checked it all out (300) where he might happen to find love; he went to the gate of the house and felt for the dilapidated wall until he touched the rotten board. As soon as he had done that (305), the lady inside noticed it. She called out: "Who is there and who is doing this?" He answered: "It is me, filled with love, not with any evil intention. You know very well who I am. Help me to get into the house." (310) The lady came up to him and welcomed him with a kiss and with an embrace, for which he had to thank her. She helped the man to come in (315). With her snow-white hands she put the board back into its original position. This way she created a secret door without the help of a carpenter.

A candle was there, burning with a bright light. Moreover, there was a jug of wine, and he also saw a cup made of silver which was precious and beautiful. The lady also had prepared good food (320). But in reality her lovely body, her rope of love, and her tender gaze imposed so much of their force upon the young man that he cared little for food and drink (330), or for any spices.

Let me cut the story short! They lay down in a wonderful bed and disarranged its blankets, full of desire, as love taught them (335). What the two did together, I want to keep silent about. Let them lie together and let them do whatever they want.

If I were sitting with my friends (340), I would take food and wine, and a lovely young lady for all kinds of sinful activities.

He who has told you this story is known as Konrad von Würzburg.

No. 14
THE KNIGHT WITH THE HAZELNUTS

The narrative motif of this tale can be traced back to Oriental literature, and was first employed in medieval Europe by the Spanish poet Petrus Alphonsus, who had converted from Judaism to Christianity, in his *Disciplina Clericalis* (ca. 1108–1110). Our tale has come down to us in three fourteenth-century manuscripts (Munich, cgm 717; Vienna, cod. 2885; Innsbruck, Tiroler Landesmuseum, Hs. FB 3200). It finds explicit parallels in the Old French fabliau *Pliçon* by Jean de Condé (d. ca.1340) and in the Middle High German *mære Schlafpelz* by Heinrich Kaufringer (ca.1400). As far as we can tell, *The Knight with the Hazelnuts* seems to have been composed in the early fourteenth century in the area of Thuringia (today central eastern Germany).

EDITION

Friedrich Heinrich von der Hagen, *Gesammtabenteuer*, 2: 273–82; cf. also Ursula Schmid, ed., *Codex Vindobonensis 2885*, 169–74.

TEXT

One must speak in good terms about women. He who does so will be blessed, because women know many tricks (are intelligent), as you will learn from an example how a knight was deceived (5). I will you tell you a true story. One day, when a knight left his wife to go hunting with his dogs, as was his custom, she immediately sent (10) for her beloved, but she did this secretly, asking him to come as soon as he received her note. When he had learned of it (15), he was very pleased and rushed to her. When he entered her room, these two secret lovers went to bed and did as their pleasure taught them (20). But what they really did, only a monk might figure out.

In the meantime, the knight was surprised by a heavy rainstorm, which forced him to return home. He thought: "Now you are getting wet: (25) go home, that would be better." At that time, just when the clouds had burst open, children had come out to collect hazelnuts. The knight approached them, who were now also seeking shelter from the rain (30) before it would come pouring down. They had already cracked open some of the hazelnuts that I have mentioned already.[1] The knight approached them and asked them to share some with him (35), which they gladly did.[2] He handed over his hat, enjoying this opportunity, and the children did not mind filling it with nuts. Then the knight rode home (40). His greyhounds ran ahead of him, and one of them scratched at the gate to the house, which greatly frightened the lover who was lying in the marital bed [with the wife]. He thought that the husband had arrived (45). When the wife heard it, she stood up quickly [and said]: "You do not have to worry." Then she said: "Dear sir, remain here quietly: this is my advice and my wish (50). The curtain is of very good quality, and nothing bad can happen to us. I will certainly and safely get you away from here in a most proper fashion. Whatever I will say, you keep quiet (55). I will help you to escape from here, believe me that."

When the husband arrived in the yard, servants immediately took his horse from him. When he got to the bedroom, she had already opened the door (60) and had sat down next to a stone. The knight was lying on the bed all by himself, hidden by the curtain. It did not take long until the husband came in (65). The wife greeted him in friendly fashion.

"Wife," he said, "what are you doing?" She answered: "I had intended to take a nap. It bothered me a great deal (70) that I was so alone. My God, what good does it do you to go hunting with your dogs, leaving me alone? (75) You would be smarter if you spent more time with me, since I soothe all your discomfort."

He replied: "I have brought you some hazelnuts." She said: "You obviously realized (80) that I have no entertainment. Now you have done well, you are indeed smart." They both sat down and cracked nuts which they picked up out of the lady's lap (85). The visitor, who was hidden behind the curtain, experienced great fear. She said: "Sir Knight, who are lying on the bed, you do not have to worry, I will help you; we do not need to bet (90) to get out of this bedroom. You are not being betrayed. As I have told you before, nothing can happen to you here. What could be the charge against you? (95) Help us crack some nuts, and no one will hurt you."

Then she took a handful of nuts and threw them behind the curtain. This eating of nuts seemed to take too long for the guest (100). The husband looked at her and said: "By God, what has happened to you? To whom are you addressing these words?"[3] She answered: "A knight is lying on our bed." (105) The husband

---

[1] This is a very strange passage in the original and would read literally: "They had already cracked open a part of the hazelnuts in their chests."

[2] This line is included only in the version used by von der Hagen in his edition, *Gesammtabenteuer.*

[3] Again a slight difference in the wording, and I am following von der Hagen's version here because the appeal to God seems quite fitting.

immediately replied: "He would not dare to await me there, if any person would indeed be there." She said: "I believe you that. You are telling me that every day (110). Now, I do not want to be guilty of it, I tell you to go there yourself. Get up and take a look who he might be. He was lying with me just a short while ago. Since you returned so quickly (115), you have robbed us of much happiness. After all, he is a courageous hero."

The husband retorted: "Truly, you are possessed by a devil, called Calumniator.[4] May God help to improve matters with you (120) and assist me in making sure that you regain your sound mind. By God, this would be really necessary! Who would be so foolhardy as to risk his death and lie down in my own bed (125), where I could catch and kill him? So help you God, be reasonable and do not vex me so badly."

Thereupon the knight's wife said: "Now get up and take a look yourself (130). You think that I have lost my mind?[5] I have all my reason together. You are deceiving yourself. I have never lied to you."[6]

He answered: "You cannot fool me, whatever you try all the time (135). You treat me like a monkey. You would like me to go there and find no one behind the curtain. Then you would laugh at me and make fun of me (140) when you are among other women. I must and want to stay here because I do not trust your words."

She said: "My words have no impact on you; one has to trust a horse when it follows its own direction [proverb] (145). But I am honestly telling you the truth, and I am ready to swear an oath; everything I have told you so far is the complete truth. But you do not dare to go to the bed: you are a coward (150). He is really lying there, the way any bold guy would do."

However much she entreated him to believe her, he never went to the bed. The man who was lying on the bed, (155) and gladly trusted the wife, did not crack any of the nuts. He rather would have gone on a pilgrimage to Saint James [Santiago de Compostella] to collect them there because he was anxious to enjoy a knight's reputation (160).

"Honestly," she said, "believe me, I have told you lies. In fact there is no other man, because I love only you. But I am going to tell you (165), if a knight were there, I would dare to get him out of here in a most proper fashion, securing his escape from this house without any loss to his honor." (170)

He answered: "How would you do that?" She: "Well, I am going to tell you. I would take you and put your head under my robe, pressing you to me (175), and

---

[4] In the Codex Vindobonensis, the husband says, instead: "You must have eaten henbane or some other herb," implying some herbal hallucinogenic.

[5] In Schmid's edition, the lady says: "Do you think that I am a ghost?"

[6] Again, this is an additional line in Schmid's edition.

then I would wrestle with you. This way I would cover your head. [Next she dem-
onstrated it to him, preparing the actual escape of her lover.] Sir Guest, now you
are permitted to take to the road: that is my command (180). Leave the house im-
mediately; I have covered his head."

Just as she had told the guest, he did not hesitate and departed right away
and disappeared without being seen by anyone (185). In this way she helped her
lover[7] to escape safely. Then she let go of her husband's head, held him by his hair
and said: "Lift your head, my love, (190) and look at me openly; understand the
joke that I played on you and forgive it me out of your goodness."

One had better take heed of evil women who know how to catch mice. Fools
deserve to be deloused with clubs.

---

[7] Whereas von der Hagen's version contains the Middle High German word "buol" for lover,
Schmid's version uses the word "ameyse," which has the same meaning, but it derives from Old
French "amis."

No. 15
ANONYMOUS: THE KNIGHT WITH THE SPARROW-HAWK

This verse narrative enjoyed considerable popularity in the fourteenth and fifteenth centuries, as testified by eleven manuscripts containing a version of the tale. In fact, this *mære* proves to be the most popular one of all representatives of this genre. We know nothing about the author, but formal aspects, such as the linguistic features, metrical forms, and the notable dependency on the famous Hartmann von Aue (ca. 1160–ca. 1200) suggest his origin from the northern Alemannic region in Germany. "The Knight with the Sparrow-Hawk" finds significant parallels in medieval European literature, specifically in the Old French fabliaux *Dulciflorie* and Garin's *De la Grue*, both early thirteenth century, and *Du Heron* from the end of the thirteenth century.

EDITION

Rolf Max Kully and Heinz Rupp, eds., *Der münch mit dem genßlein*, 59–71. For a historical-critical, but not necessarily better, edition, see Klaus Grubmüller, *Novellistik des Mittelalters*, 568–88.

TEXT

Just as I have been told in full truth, I am going to tell you a story the same way, and I am going to read it to you as I heard it being read. Once there was a cloister, as I have been told, (5) which was wealthy and well endowed. The nuns who lived there, both the old and the young ones, sang God's praise. They celebrated mass and happily sang in the choir (10) all day long, and they did needlework with golden thread, competing against each other as best they could. At times, when they were not singing (15), they did all kinds of textile work, including weaving. Each of them would have been ashamed if she did not have anything to do. Some painted, and some copied texts (20), each working according to her skills and abilities.

It was, as I have been told, their law and custom never to let (25) any man enter the convent, whatever the circumstances might be. This allowed them to stay in the convent, and not one of them ever left the monastery (30), except for those who had special duties. Those who were not yet wise in years had to stay inside and were educated by a teacher. The young novices practiced singing and reading (35), how to observe the convent rules, how to speak and how to walk, how to bow before the choir and pay respect, just as the convent rules demanded. They had such sweet lips (40) that God could not refuse to fulfill what they asked and begged him, acting in good trust (45).

At that time there was a beautiful virgin. If she had lived anywhere else and would have been seen by people they would have to admit (50) that she was without any faults indeed in her appearance and in her mind, and she completely deserved this recognition (55) as one who fulfilled all expectations one might have in a woman. There was only one thing that she lacked: that is that she was entirely innocent about people and knew nothing about their ways or their customs (60) as they were practiced outside. After all, she had spent her whole life up to the fifteenth year in the convent (65). She did not care at all about the material goods in the outside world. She lived in her simplemindedness fully in accordance with the rules of the convent in which she had been raised (70).

One day this virgin took a walk on the wall surrounding the convent near the main gate (75) where the road passed by. At that moment a man came riding along who proved to be a knight both in his bodily appearance and in his outfit. He held a sparrow-hawk on his hand (80). When he came close to her, she greeted him in friendly fashion, which pleased his heart. She said: "My dear lord (85), what is the name of this little thing which you hold on your hand? I have no idea what it is and would like to ask you to enlighten me." He answered: "It is a sparrow-hawk."

Now listen what happened next. She spoke to him in most friendly terms: "Please allow me to ask you, and do not be cross with me, my dear lord (95), have you brought the bird from afar?" "No, my lady," he said. "Dear lord, please let me know what kind of bird this is (100). Its claws are so yellow, its eyes are beautiful and round, its plumage is so smooth, and if only its beak were straight, it would not be marred by any shortcomings (105). I can well imagine that it might sing sweetly. Whoever the lady might be to whom you are carrying it, she will always grant you her favor; it is a beautiful bird indeed." (110)

The knight clearly noticed by the virgin's words that she was truly inexperienced and foolish. Again he told her (115): "It is called a sparrow-hawk." Then he said: "I am willing to sell it, and you can easily purchase it if you are willing to pay for it." She replied: "We rarely receive any spending money (120) here in the convent. Could you think of anything else you might want to have in return for the deal, since I do not want to miss this opportunity because I would love to own the bird." (125) He said: "My dear young lady, since you desire so much to make this purchase, I am willing to accept your offer and am prepared to give you the bird in exchange for your *minne* [love]. I would not be opposed to this arrangement." (130)

She was very pleased with his words and replied: "I do not know what you want, though you have mentioned it, calling it *minne* (135) with which I am, unfortunately, unfamiliar. I really wonder what it might be. I have nothing else in my chest than two pictures [of saints?], three needles, one pair of scissors, (140) a new hair-band, four dresses, and a good psalter. I have never acquired anything else in my life (145). I will let you choose among them. Even if my aunt will be angry with me, I will still have this bird."

He answered: "Virtuous maid, your body is so delightful (150) I trust to find it [*minne*] in yourself, if I were allowed to search for it. If you do not mind, I will take you down from the wall." (155). "But how will I get back up there?" said the young woman. The knight was mightily pleased with her words, helped her down the wall and led her straight away (160) into an orchard. He carefully looked around to see whether anyone could observe what they were going to do. He attached his horse tightly (165) to a branch, and did the same with the sparrow-hawk. Then he took off his armor and sat down next to her in the grass [clover]. He did not hurt the good maid (170); instead he looked for *minne* until he had found it and made her familiar with it. He hugged her and kissed her as much as he desired, and then looked for *minne* once again (175). Then the young woman said: "Take this *minne* with you completely, so that I pay you in full and do not cheat you. Understand what I am telling you (180): he who acquires such a good item and then sinfully cheats [the vendor] by not paying the full price commits a grave misdeed. Take as much *minne* as you please (185). I have carefully counted [and find] that I have not granted you enough as payment, so take to your heart's content. Since I have to pay with *minne*, I trust that I will be able to pay properly (190). I am ready to pay every penny." Again the attractive and courtly knight took the *minne* until he thought to himself that his sparrow-hawk had been well remunerated. In his heart he also knew that never before (195) had any of his birds of prey been paid for better. Then he helped her get up on to the wall (200) and said good-bye to her. He rode off and left her behind. She also returned [to the convent] and was happy about her purchase.

She approached her aunt and said: "My very dear aunt (205), I have bought this wonderful bird for very little, without one penny. A knight gave it to me—may his life be blessed (210)—I allowed him to look for something called *minne* as often as he liked. I have learned to understand what it is and did not mind at all (215) that he searched for it often. He was so skillful in his effort! What a pity that the convent has never hired such a searcher! I will always suffer heavily (220) if I am to be deprived of his art for long; yet I will be happy about this experience for ever."

Then she addressed her aunt once again: "We have so many riches here that it is just unfair (225) that we are not allowed to acquire something that a person offers for sale. If this sale might be too expensive, we all should throw in our own money (230). I have never acquired anything so delightful and will help us all to purchase it."

The old woman began to chastise her, tore out her hair, and beat her as punishment for having made this purchase (235). She had good reason to lament to God, and she almost killed her with this beating, so that she fell down twice. [She screamed:] "Now you have turned into a woman (240); in your stupidity you have lost your honor. You will never regain the rank of a virgin, and you should be ashamed of it!" (245) She was filled with great wrath, and she thrashed and beat the young woman many times.

Once this was over, the young woman was very submissive (250), and thought to herself how she could make up for her guilt and appease her aunt. She thought about it many times in her heart for eight days (255). Secretly she sneaked out to the wall and sat down at the same place again, looking down the wall to see whether she might be so lucky as (260) to espy the knight another time, which was the only thought she had in her mind. Not long afterwards the knight came riding by on his horse. Politely she approached him (265): "Please help me down from the wall and give me back my *minne*. Indeed, my aunt was so furious because of this little bird (270) and said that I have lost my honor because of the sparrow-hawk, and here also my virginity. Now, take me down from here, give me back my *minne* (275), and you, take back your bird."

He said: "Young woman, this shall be as you wish." He took her down to him and put her down on the grass and did the same with her as before. Again he looked for the *minne* (280) as well as he could. Then she said: "If I had permission, I would buy two birds every day, but my aunt would say (285) that I would have piled even more shame on myself. Therefore, do a better job and help me to turn into a virgin again as I was before. Perhaps you think that you might hurt me; you might intend to remit some of my debt (290), but you should not worry about it. Make me into a virgin again, and you will not hear any complaints from me. I will contend with everything. However you put me down, or whatever you do with me (295), my aunt will have to let go her anger when she hears the news."

He paid her back her *minne* twice and said: "Now I want to depart from here (300), may God protect you well!" She said: "You will not go away from here like that! Thinking that I am naïve, you want to cheat me?" She began to fight with him (305). [She said]: "I won't let you go: so far you have paid me back only twice, whereas before you took my *minne* three times. It would be an unfair deal if you were to sneak away this way (310). You will have to pay me back the third *minne* as well. If you want to fight against it, my anger will follow you forever."

"Very well, Lady, so I will do it (315)," said the virtuous man. What she said did not matter to him, but he granted her wish as she requested. Then he helped her get back up on the wall and departed from her (320). He rode away and left her behind.

She went back to the convent and was very happy. She said to her aunt: "My dear beloved aunt, please let your wrath go away (325). I have made everything all right again because I have regained my virginity. That was the reason why you were so angry with me and why you said that I had lost my honor and my virginity (330) for a sparrow-hawk. While you were sleeping around noontime, the lord to whom I had given my *minne* fairly repaid me. I would be able to walk for miles now without any help and any walking stick [so much have I recovered everything]. It was really strange that you were so angry with me and said that he had taken away my honor when he took my *minne* (340). Even had he never returned to this part of the world, I would have survived what he did to me. I will be thankful to him for ever since he treated me so well. May God grant him to travel joyfully! (345) I wish him well, as behooves me, since he would be an enrichment to our convent."

The abbess, who was very sad about what she had to say, responded: "Whatever anyone might say or do [about it] (350), you will have to bear a bad conscience. If the damage had been limited to only one, it would have been a small one. When the first time had happened, I should have let it go (355). Since I did not do that, I will have to let go my anger."

Those who listened to my account should pay attention to my advice: he who discovers a fire (360) should be careful not to be burned by it. Whether he is a man or a woman, as long as he knows how to discriminate between good and evil, this will help him very much and will protect his honor (365).

Herewith the story comes to its conclusion. It dealt with the sparrow-hawk, the fortunate knight, and the happy maid who abandoned the rules of her monastic order in exchange for the sparrow-hawk, and thus lost her virginity.

No. 16
Heinrich Kaufringer: The Search for the Happily Married Couple

We are not really sure who Heinrich Kaufringer might have been, though he refers to himself by name at the end of three verse narratives contained in a collection of seventeen texts of comparable material in a Munich (Bayerische Staatsbibliothek, cgm 270) manuscript, copied in 1464. We know of two citizens of Landsberg am Lech west of Munich, father and son, who shared the same name. The older of the two is documented as rector of the Landsberg parish church since 1369 and died in 1404; the younger is only mentioned briefly, but not after 1404, perhaps because he did not assume a significant position within the church or the city administration. There is no way to determine which of these two persons might have created these verse narratives, if both did not work on them either separately or together.

EDITION

Klaus Grubmüller, ed., *Novellistik des Mittelalters*, 768–96.

TEXT

I have often heard an old proverb that a man and his wife should have two souls and one body together (5). What happens to one, whether it be good or bad, happens also to both of them. They are supposed to be in such a union that if one of them wants something full-heartedly (10) and really takes pleasure in it, then the other should agree to it as well. This might then be called a pure life and can truly be counted as a perfect marriage (15).

I would like to tell you a true story. Once there was a rich burgher who enjoyed great respect and honor. He was generous and high-spirited and descended from a good family (20). He was respectable and virtuous and enjoyed much honor. He lived a grand life. His heart was filled with great joy when his good friends (25) visited him at home. He liked it very much to have them with him since he did not enjoy missing their company. He was married to a virtuous woman whom he loved as much as his own life (30). She commanded much honor and respect, and was blessed with countless virtues. She happily fulfilled his wishes, but the husband had to suffer much sorrow from his good wife (35) because he was so generous and enjoyed company at home. She was angry with him because she was rather miserly. When her husband let her know (40) that he wanted to host a company, she chastised him. This pained the husband a lot. If he pulled towards one direction, she pulled toward the other. She was too miserly, he was too generous (45). But I do not blame the wife because she was submissive to him in all other respects.

One day her husband was sitting all by himself and ruminated about the following matter (50): "How is it possible that everywhere here in the city my wife is praised by all people for having infinite virtues (55), honor, and respectability? They even say about her that she is free of all instability. To me this seems to be a foolish idea because she causes me sorrow and suffering (60) with her evil miserliness. The entire city assumes, and says so as well, that she entirely follows my wishes. In reality she is totally opposed to me, indeed, more than anyone knows about (65). I have suffered from it secretly for a long time, and I cannot tolerate it any longer. We are not of one body as everyone says and thinks about us (70). In fact, I will not neglect to search and also to find, anywhere in the entire world, two virtuous and pure married people who are so much of one mind that each of them agrees with the other (75) whatever she or he might think of, without them ending in a fight and struggle. I am determined to carry out this plan (80), as I have conceived it."

The man immediately prepared himself for a long journey and took a lot of travel provisions with him, since he had immeasurable wealth. Officially he said that he wanted to do business as a merchant (85), trusting his good fortune. Then this virtuous and respectable man rode off, together with a servant, and went to see many major cities.

The way he traveled (90) was that whenever he reached a bigger city he did not mind spending considerable time there trying to find what he was looking for (95), as far as this was possible, that is, two married people determined fully by the same mind and attitude who did not suffer from conflicts, fights, or bickering. He went traveling so long (100) that he consumed a great amount of his money, and yet it was not granted to him to discover anywhere in those days such good and pure married people [as he was looking for] (105). Nevertheless, he did not want to return home; instead he wanted rather to use up all his money first.

Thus he spent four years. In the fifth year he arrived at a magnificent city (110) which was great and wealthy. Here as well he intended to spend some of his travel money. He lived for about half a year with a rich burgher (115) who was loyal and very trustworthy. He was married to a virtuous wife. In words, in actions, and in their minds they treated everything the same. No one observed any fighting or conflict between them (120). I must truly tell you, the worthy traveler was very pleased about it. He said to his servant: "Indeed, I have found here (125) what I have been seeking for many years. Now we can ride home."

When the host realized that the guest wanted to depart, he said very politely (130) and in private to his guest: "I beg you, my dear sir, and consider it as just a friendly gesture, that you let me know what your business has been here (135). You cannot find many business affairs here which might be fruitful for your country. Therefore my mind tells me that you are looking for adventure here. My heart would really be pleased (140) if it could learn right now what it might be, and this request comes in full friendship and without any evil cunning." Immediately the guest answered him: "In secret I will let you know what my intentions are (145). Back home I am married to a proper, virtuous, and good wife. All my possessions are well protected and taken care of by her. She complies with all my wishes; (150) in only one aspect does she fail. I am very unhappy with one fault in her: she is a little too miserly. She chastises me all the time for trying hard to gain public recognition [by being generous and hospitable] (155). In this matter she is very different from me. This is the reason why I had to leave home, because I thought to myself that I would never return home until I found two virtuous married people (160) who fully share the same ideas. These I have now discovered, in the fifth year, best represented by you and your wife (165). Therefore I will not stay any longer and will prepare to go home." Thereupon the host said right away: "You ought to stay here one more day with me (170); then I will let you know what the shared life between my wife and myself is really like." The guest replied: "I will happily stay, my dear sir." (175)

The host invited his friends and enjoyed great festivities with them. No one was bored. Many musicians performed, and the group was accompanied by many beautiful ladies (180). One could hear beautiful songs, and later the women danced gracefully. The host's wife was very joyful, and her heart leaped for happiness. The guest was very pleased with it (185). Truly, I must tell you, they celebrated all day until late at night. Once the party had come to a conclusion and everyone had gone home, the host began to speak (190) with his esteemed guest.

He said: "You have seen my wife act today as if she were in a good mood, and that was the case (195). But now I want to let you know the true reason for it, which was also the intention why I held you back and why I celebrated this festival with my wife. Often pain follows happiness (200), and after joy follow heartfelt laments. Similarly my wife has spent the present day full of joys, from which she could profit much. But now you will have to observe (205) and witness yourself and understand most drastically that this joy cannot last for ever. Afterwards painful complaints always ensue for the wife, as she has brought it upon herself."

Thereupon he quickly addressed the woman[/wife] (210) and said: "Now bring your drinking vessel. Then I want to pour your St. John's love drink [a memorial or good-bye drink] which I have right here. Afterwards we can go to sleep."

The woman became very frightened at his words (215). "I will never bring out the drinking vessel here," she said, "you can believe that! I will rather suffer the pain of death. What are your intentions with me today? Allow me to drink it (220) in your presence only in the bedroom, my dear husband, as I have been used to do it."

The husband did not grant her this wish; instead he went and brought the drinking vessel himself and placed it in front of the bashful woman (225), which hurt her a lot. She was deeply ashamed in front of the guest whose presence intensified her embarrassment. The vessel was the skull of a human, into which the host poured (230) the white wine without any hesitation. Then he said to her: "See, now take and drink what I brought you: the love of St. John." The wife did not fight against it because she did not dare to oppose her husband (235). She drank from the cup very sorrowfully.

The host then spoke to the guest: "Sir, this is the misfortune that I have to witness every night. Whenever I want to go to sleep (240), my wife, who has no other choice, has to drink from this human skull which I tore out of the head of a priest. I had found him lying with my wife while he made love with her (245). I killed him and secretly buried him so that no one knows of his whereabouts. I took his skull as a pledge (250), and my wife has to drink from it. For five years now she has had to go through this process of penance every night. I have also decided that I will never absolve her from it (255); she will have to perform this penance for the rest of her life, and no one will be able to change that."

When the guest had heard these words, he went to his servant (260) and said: "Let us not stay here; we must ride off: the time has not yet come as I had thought previously that we could return home." (265) He immediately said good-bye [to the host]. Onward they traveled. Honestly, I must tell you, the further the man got on his journey, the less he heard of that (270) which his heart desired so strongly. In this way he rode all over the country until he had spent the thousand gold coins that he had in his purse, and so finally he had only a little money left (275).

Then he took a rest in a large and broad city. There he selected an innkeeper who was powerful and also rich. To him the life that the latter and his wife enjoyed (280) seemed to be equal. He thought that he had [at last] found two souls in one body in this woman and her husband. He was very pleased with their life [together] (285). He studied them carefully to see whether he could observe anything to the contrary. He was even ready to go home because he had found two married people who were unified (290) in a harmonious marriage. Each of them loved the other in full loyalty without any doubt.

When the innkeeper noticed that the guest wanted to depart (295), he said: "Dear guest, I like you very much. You display courteous and decent behavior. It seems to me that you are looking for an adventure. Let me know what it might be. I am a man here (300) of such family connections and power that I might easily help you in this matter here in this town and its surroundings. If you have any pressing issue, then let me know it in confidence (305); no one will find out about it."

The guest answered him politely: "I am going to tell you my secret intention. I am pursuing a strange adventure. At home I have a lovely wife (310) who does everything according to my wishes. Each of us appreciates what the other is doing. We agree with it fully in our mind. But there is one problem with her (315) because she is really too miserly. This grieves me considerably. Truly, I am telling you: at home I enjoy much power but I rode away (320) and went to distant lands. I have spent probably thousands of gold coins because I cannot find a woman and her husband who would be entirely unified in their mind (325). Instead I encounter nothing but bickering and fighting, wherever I have traveled. The one pulls this way, the other the opposite way. I had intended not to return home (330) until I would have found two married people with whom I would have observed no disagreement between them. I have been searching for this by now for more than six years (335). Only now have I realized that I have discovered this ideal couple in you and your wife. I do not observe anything else between you but that you are friendly to each other (340), both day and night. I am so happy and joyful about it. Therefore I have prepared to return home for sure, home to my wife and my house (345); after all, I have been away for a long time."

The host then said to the guest: "You have to suffer very little trouble with your wife, as you describe it. I will tell you of my heart-felt suffering (350) in complete confidence, if you keep quiet about it and do not tell anyone about it. Promise me this right here, because I do not want to let anyone [else] know about it." (355) The guest did not hesitate and promised him that he would not divulge this account to anyone, because he was loyal and honest.

The host then took his guest and led him into his house (360), down to a deep and wide cellar. In a hidden corner there was a wide room with stone walls, which the host opened for his guest. A large peasant lived in it (365) who was terrible to look at, strong and evil. He was locked up with a strong and solid chain so that he could not leave. He stood there looking as if a stormy breeze (370) had disheveled his hair, and he appeared to be very threatening. When the guest saw the peasant he asked the host: "This is a most strange matter here (375). What does this frightful peasant mean, whom you keep a prisoner?"

The host responded without hesitation: "Dear guest, I will let you know how my life truly is (380). Pay close attention. I come from a good family, and so does my wife. We might well be the most noble family here in the city, be assured of that (385), in terms of both our birth and our wealth. But my wife does not comport herself according to what would befit her, since she is filled with unchaste desire [literally: full of unchastity]. This unchastity has driven her around in the city (390), and has cast shame on her family. My honor was also robbed from me, and I had to suffer for her evil nature. Both old and young deemed me to be too weak because of my wife's failing (395). When I realized her shortcoming and that she did not intend to combat it, I acted like one who commands dignity and honor. I rode to a distant country (400) where no one knew me. I found this strong peasant there. With the help of my friends and servants I forcefully kidnapped him. This happened all in secret (405), and no one heard or saw whereto he had disappeared. I transported him secretly here into my house without any difficulties. There he has to stay a prisoner (410) as long as my wife is alive. She visits him always whenever she wants to do her evil thing. He plays the game of love with her until she is satisfied (415) and has no further demands.

"Now everyone assumes indeed that she has really improved, so now she is appreciated and valued publicly. But my honor is deeply hurt (420), in secret and silently. Good wine and food that I enjoy every day I myself bring to the peasant for his dinner (425). I take better care of him, by my honor, than of myself in order that he may sleep with my wife so that she will be sexually satisfied and does not look for the pleasure of sex elsewhere (430), as she used to do before. That had brought shame and disgrace upon me in the past. I tell you truly, this torture with the peasant I have carried out for ten years (435). During this time my wife has not had sex with any other man. Dear guest, look at my children whom I have under my care. Everyone assumes (440) that they are my own. This is the cause of great pain for me because they are the peasant's offspring, all six of my children."

When the guest had listened to these words (445), he was deeply horrified. The host's suffering grieved him badly. The latter then spoke to him again: "I advise you, honestly, do not stay away any longer (450) from your virtuous and good wife. You behave badly toward her indeed. She does not deserve to be treated this way because she is not guilty of any disloyalty. Her miserliness cannot be reprimanded (455). If you intend to travel around in the country, you will squander your wealth and lose it entirely before you will find, believe me that (460), what you have been looking for.

"No one is completely perfect. The devil likes to sow his seeds [of discontent] among married people, which makes it hardly possible (465) for them to live together without any strife."

The guest immediately followed the host's advice. He decided to ride home as the host had recommended to him. In friendship he said good-bye, but he was very sad [for him]. He gave the one horse in place of payment for food to make the journey home. The servant had to walk on foot (475). The noble man thus rode off, and soon they both got home. The honorable and chaste wife was happy about her husband's return. From then on he did not any longer oppose (480) her parsimonious life-style.

Often he thought of the places where he had been before; he thought of the drinking vessel and also of the giant peasant (485) who was held by chains. When he carefully considered everything, he realized that both their lives which he and his wife enjoyed were free of shame and suffering (490). He accepted it when she got angry with him because of his excessive generosity [literally: carried the crown of generosity], and tolerated her chiding.

Therefore let me give you this advice (495). Every good man ought to disregard this little shortcoming of his wife if he cannot discover any other blemish in her character except for her miserliness (500). He should be resigned to it and should not cause her any pain or irritate her since it is the least shortcoming a woman might suffer from (505). More I am not going to tell you.

No. 17
Heinrich Kaufringer:
The Innocent Murderess

For biographical and literary-historical background concerning Kaufringer, see the introduction to the previous narrative.

EDITION

Klaus Grubmüller, ed., *Novellistik des Mittelalters*, 798–838.

TEXT

God never lets it happen that an innocent person is abandoned by His fatherly protection. He helps him all the time and without fail in suffering and pain. When a man is convinced (5) that he can fully rely on God and entrust Him with all his suffering, know for sure that God will never abandon him and will always stand at his side (10). This I want to illustrate for you with an account of how a virgin had to suffer much and how she had to bear much pain, which caused her heartfelt grief, though she was innocent and without any guilt (15). God in His grace helped her and rescued her from all her suffering.

This virgin was truly chaste, pious, pretty, and tender, and she descended from a high-ranking family (20). She held the rank of a countess and ruled over a country. She had a good brother, a high-minded noble knight who was a true hero in his physical prowess (25). Not far away there was a king who was noble, young, and rich. He did not find a lady anywhere who held the same aristocratic rank and whom he could have married (30), except for the good countess. The king began to fancy her and desired to win her as his wife. The young count immediately granted him this wish (35) and married his sister to the king, who loved her as himself. When the marriage was agreed upon, everyone said (40) that they were both equally virtuous, noble, and enjoyed the same rank. They were highly praised for their reputation.

The king had [at his court] a knight (45) who was full of rancor. He in turn had a servant who was evil and cunningly said the following words to his lord:

"Listen, my dear sir, what I am going to tell you is true. My lord the king has agreed to a bad marriage. The virgin has not been without a man until now (55). She has had more sexual experiences than four evil women. I will arrange it in no time that she will fulfill your wish (60), and then you will notice that she is completely bad. If you follow my advice you will enjoy a great experience." When the knight heard these words (65)—he was careless and foolish—he developed evil thoughts. He said: "My dear friend, help me and give me your advice on how I should proceed in this matter (70) in order to realize my desire. After all, the king intends to lie down with the noble maid without any delay tomorrow night and celebrate his wedding with her (75). If I were so fortunate as to enjoy her beforehand I would be exceedingly happy."

The servant said: "Sir, listen to me, I want to give you good advice (80) so that you will embrace the virgin tonight, as I have planned it. Her brother, the young count, will celebrate tonight, together with his court and all his people, (85) pre-nuptial festivities with his [future] brother-in-law, the noble king. They plan to deliberate together how to carry out the wedding honorably (90) and most effectively. At that time the maid will be alone in her strong castle. No one is guarding her tonight except the watchman. I want to ride with you to the forest outside of the castle and stay there hidden until the early morning (100). You will leave your horse with me and walk on foot up to the mighty castle. Let the guardsman know and tell him in pleasant words (105): 'Guardsman, may God give you a reward, tell your noble maid to let the king enter because he wants to ask her for advice which would be good for her and him.' (110) She will not deny you this request. When it dawns, then return to me right at the spot where you left me behind."

The knight was pleased with this suggestion (115). They both got ready and rode across the land toward the fortress. Soon they reached a dense forest (120) not far from the castle. At that moment they saw a large group of people approaching them on horseback, equipped with shields and lances and knightly armor (125). It was the noble and powerful king and his brother-in-law, the good count. They rode happily out of the young count's castle intending to spend the night (130) at the king's castle, and the group included all the knights and squires. The [afore-mentioned] knight and his servant turned away to the side so that no one noticed them (135), until the entire group had passed them on the road. They did not tarry any longer and turned to the splendid castle. The knight was in good spirits (140) because he had fully realized that no one who could cause him trouble was in the castle. Now the sun set and disappeared (145), and the night arrived, a time when people like to take things that do not rightfully belong to them. He who does evil as a thief likes the dark night (150) and hates the bright day.

The servant stayed quietly in the forest, keeping the two horses. The knight stealthily walked to the moat (155) and called out: "Guard, good man, tell your noble lady that she should let me in. I am the king and stand here alone. I need to see the chaste maid (160) to get her advice and also to tell her something that is important for us both. If she denies me this request now, then we both will without fail experience suffering." (165) The guard immediately told the news to the noble maid. She was very much frightened at these words and was uncertain what to do (170). "If I allow the lord to come in, I will not have any power to refuse him anything he might want to do which could harm my honor. [However,] I, a noble and honorable lady, must obey him (175); I have no choice but to live with him and die with him because I am engaged to him. But if I do not allow him to enter, and if he then will suffer such pain (180), as he had said, he will avenge this on me forever." She felt torn two ways, and was deeply concerned for her own honor and worried about great damage that might affect her in the future (185).

Finally she decided to let him in, whatever might happen to her. She went to the gatekeeper and got the keys from him (190). She asked him to accompany her secretly. He had to lower the drawbridge. The knight was allowed in because he appeared to be the noble king. She led him quickly (195) to her room and said: "My dear lord, what might be your business that you have come here by yourself? I am deeply frightened." (200) He answered her in friendly fashion: "Maid, believe me that I am going to tell you the truth, and I'll assure you upon my oath that I am passionately in love with you (205) and burn to be with you since you have been pledged to me as my wife. If I cannot embrace you, lovely creature, tonight, my life will be wasted (210) and I will have to die. But if you will obey me without delay, I tell you upon my honor that I will reward you (215) for ever." The maid answered: "Sir, why are you doing this? I have clearly understood that we will be in great joy (220) tomorrow night without doubt. We will have our wedding in a very short time. I trust that you will leave me in peace (225) and wait. This is more appropriate for my honor instead of letting you fulfill your desire with me."

What can I say? He begged the maid so strongly (230) that she complied with his wish. She thought that it was her beloved fiancé, the noble and powerful king. But he was not at all like him. He made the virgin a woman (235) when he caressed her body and spent the time full of joy with her. But she also experienced much happiness and gave him much pleasure as is proper for a good woman (240) when she is in bed with her husband. She tenderly embraced him with her naked white arms. She pressed him to her full of love, and she did this without any cunning (245). The knight, however, reacted to her behavior in a bad way. Foolishly he said: "My servant has spoken truly that the king has indeed (250) married an evil, dishonorable woman." The woman immediately asked: "What did you say?" He said: "Dear beloved wife, do not be angry with me (255), I have become foolish as a result of my sleepiness. More I cannot say." He wished he could have taken back his words because he had spoken too much. I tell you honestly (260), his words hurt the beautiful lady.

After this heavy exercise the knight fell asleep. What did the woman do? She quietly left him (265) and lit a candle and returned with it to the man. She looked into his face and soon recognized that he was not the king (270). She was deeply horrified that she had lost her honor in this way through the evil man. She went away filled with grief, anger, and with much commotion, (275) and looked for a strong and sharp knife which she took with her to the bedroom. Quickly she severed the knight's head from his body, which was the pledge he had to leave behind (280).

But now she was in trouble and went to the gatekeeper who had let the knight in. She said: "My dear friend, help me in this terrible emergency (285). I will give you so much gold for the rest of your life that you will be rich for ever. The knight who came here tonight and whom you and I let in (290), and who called himself the king, has deceived me badly. He wanted to rob me of my honor, for which he paid with his life. I cut off his head (295). I beg you now with all my might that you help me throw the corpse into the well. The corpse is too heavy for me. I will go with you (300) and will drop the head into the well. Do not say a word about it to anyone, and I will reward you so well that you can lead a better life until your death." (305)

Quickly the gatekeeper replied: "I fully understand now that the knight has hurt you, he has slept with you. If you are willing to reward me by sharing your body with me (310), I will be ready to do what you have asked me. But if you do not let me sleep with you, your begging will be for nought." The lady said: "Do not speak thus! (315) I will make you happy and raise you to [the rank of] a lord." He answered: "My dear lady, I will not comply with your request. I will not renounce my desire (320); I must first have sex with you. Then I will do what I must and what you asked me to do. If you reward me this way, then this is a better payment (325) than your silver and your gold." Whatever the lady asked the servant, he would not do it, unless she allowed him to sleep with her. She was deeply grieved (330).

What can I tell you? She had no alternative and had to allow the gatekeeper to take her noble body for his sexual needs. He did with her what he lusted for (335), just as his heart desired. After he had committed this evil deed, the lady urged the gatekeeper and took him to the bedroom. He picked up the dead body (340) and heaved him onto his shoulder. The lady carried the head. Then both went to the well. She insisted and said to the gatekeeper (345): "Now bend over carefully and let the corpse drop into the water without making any noise, so that the guard does not hear the splash (350)." The gatekeeper followed her order, and bent over with the corpse so that he could let it fall into the well silently (355). The lady was clever and smart, and lifted him up by his feet and threw him into the water, this traitor of a gatekeeper—bravo! This was his reward for love (360).

He immediately drowned at the bottom of the water. She herself threw down the [severed] head.

She did not tarry there (365) and quickly returned to her chamber. The bed linens were stained red with blood. She was deeply worried how to clean it all up so that no one would notice anything (370). She washed and worked hard and did not get any rest until dawn. She made every effort until she managed to arrange it all so that no one could learn anything (375) about this event.

Now, as the day had begun, the [evil knight's] servant waited in the forest not far away from the castle. He looked hard to see when his lord (380) would return from the castle and come back to him as they had agreed upon. He worried about his lord. He waited in the meadow almost until noon (385), when the young count came home riding through the forest, well armored, together with his entourage. He wanted to get quickly to his castle and to his chaste sister (390). When they had come closer and discovered the servant who held a knightly horse with his hand, they rushed up to him and questioned him about (395) what his business was there. Fearfully he tried to avoid them. He was neither smart nor intelligent in this situation because he did not harbor good intentions. They accused him of being evil and miserable, (400) and accused him openly of having stolen the two horses. They beat him strongly and hard, and then they hanged him from a tree branch for everyone to see (405). He choked so badly that he soon died. He had earned his death because he had given evil advice which had led to the knight's death (410) and the gatekeeper's death. Moreover, the maid had also fallen into a dire situation because of his advice. She had lost the greatest honor which God had granted her (415). This was the result of the evil advice this scoundrel had given. Let him hang there.

The count cheerfully arrived at his mighty castle (420) and told his sister about this event. She thought about it but did not say anything, because she well understood the connection among all these occurrences. Then the count said: (425) "Sister, you must prepare yourself now without any delay. We must go to the wedding. The king is going to be married and has chosen you as his wife (430). Today you will be his bride. Be ready, my sister." She became very frightened because she had lost her honor since she had been cheated by an evil man (435). Nevertheless the sorrowful and unhappy lady prepared herself immediately, together with all her maids, and so did the count with his entourage. The maid was brought to the king (440) at court with all the expected honors. The noble king was very happy about it and welcomed her respectfully and in friendly fashion. The young woman, however, felt deep pain. Whereas everyone else was filled with happiness (445), the lady had to lament bitterly and secretly in her heart. She greatly lamented her grief and pain to the mighty God. Although she had much sorrow in her heart (450), her behavior did not betray anything of her grief.

Then the dinner was ready. The king and the pretty lady, the count and many noble knights (455), and also many beautiful women were placed at the table. They were served in large quantities with venison and fish, and whatever else was appropriate for such a meal (460). They fared well and had enough food. Much was left over and was carried away. After they had eaten plentifully and the tables had been cleared (465), many musicians with trombones and flutes played for their entertainment and sang many songs.

Afterwards the king went to bed. The count took his sister (470) and led her, holding her with both his arms, to the chamber. When she got to the bed, she quickly turned to one of her maids (475) whom she trusted most. She said: "Send everyone away!" This was done immediately. The lady and her maid, and the noble king (480) remained there alone; all the others were told to leave. The king lay on the bed. The maid saw to the light. The queen said to her: (485) "Accompany me outside, I need to use the bathroom." They did so immediately. They both left the room with the light (490). The queen said politely: "Listen to what I will have to ask of you. I trust you especially; please be grateful in return. When we return to the room (495) to the king, my lord, put out the light immediately and be mindful of all the good things that I have ever done for you. Lie down on the bed (500) next to my dear lord and stay there until he has fulfilled his desire with you to his satisfaction. I promise to give you as reward endless amounts (505) of gold and silver, upon my honor, enough to fill your chests, but honestly promise me in return that you will leave the bed right away (510) when I will ask you for it tonight."

The maid did not object, and right away promised the queen loyally and without cunning (515) to do everything she had asked of her. Then they entered the chamber and put out the light. The maid did not hesitate at all (520) and lay down with the king without saying a word, just in the right manner, as if she were the queen. The queen stood nearby and heard well what happened (525). The king embraced the maid and made love with her just as he desired. He held her tightly to him and made the virgin a woman (530). The queen heard everything well because she was not far away, standing quietly in the chamber.

When the king had satisfied his desire with the maid (535), the queen became nervous. She waited restlessly until the king had fallen asleep and began to snore. Then she did not hesitate any longer (540) and approached the bed. She asked the maid to leave the bed as she had promised her to do. But the maid did not want to do it, (545) and was not willing to make peace with the queen or to speak with her in a friendly manner. The queen became deeply frightened. Once again she begged the maid (550) not to behave so badly and to stay steadfastly loyal as she had promised her. But whatever the queen begged or said, it did not help at all (555). The maid did not want to leave; she wanted to be queen herself, which was a great pain for the [real] queen and big trouble. She had never experienced greater sorrow (560). She walked around in the chamber and would have almost lost her mind and gone crazy. Then she decided to try (565) her luck once again, and returned to the bed as before and begged the maid even more not to commit such a crime against her. In response the maid began to shout so loud (570) that it resounded in the entire chamber. She spoke with a loud voice, disregarding the danger that the king might wake up. But he was so deeply asleep that he did not hear anything (575) of their verbal exchange.

The queen had to give up the idea of being with the king, though she would have loved to lie with the noble king. She no longer dared to ask [the maid] to let her be with the king (580). Many thoughts crossed her mind. As she was standing there heavy with sadness and a grieving heart, she heard well that the maid had also fallen asleep (585). She carefully thought to herself to cause her pain as well. She stealthily and quietly went to the kitchen and lit a light without making any noise (590). With this she returned to the chamber and set fire to it in all four corners, making it go up in flames. Then she rushed to the bed where the king lay and slept (595). She took off her dress and stood there stark naked. She embraced the king and pulled him off the bed. She shouted: "Get up, my dear husband! (600) We must escape from here if we do not want to die in this house from the fire, which is burning hard and fierce." The king jumped up immediately (605) and thanked his wife because she rescued him from the danger. They barely managed to run through the door out of the chamber. The queen locked it with the bolt (610) and left with the king. The maid in the chamber burned to fine ash. Losing her life was the proper reward (615) for her great disloyalty.

The king and the noble lady loved each other and lived well together. She was very loyal toward the noble king (620), her lord. He was equally loyal to her, this noble and beautiful lady.

After they had lived together for thirty-two years in this way (625), as I have been told, the noble king one day rested with his head in her lap and fell asleep. The lady mused about many things (630) and was filled with ruefulness for having taken the knight's life, and she felt sorry for him, and so for having killed the gatekeeper and the maid, and that the disloyal servant (635) also had to die. This all returned to her mind, and she began to cry so hard that the tears dropped onto the king's face. He [woke up] and said: "My dear wife, (640), tell me, what has happened to you? Indeed, I have never seen you filled with so much sadness. Let me know, good woman, who has done harm to you? (645) He will have to pay for it with his life." The lady could not hold back. She was filled with so much grief that her husband decided to get to the bottom of her problem and solve it (650). But he had to promise her not to be wrathful or angry with her. This he pledged her for good.

The lady began to tell him (655) how the noble knight had come to her at night cunningly pretending to be the king, then had slept with her, and finally betrayed himself (660) through the words that he had spoken to her and for which he had to give his head as a payment. Then she told the king how she had been raped [forced] by the gatekeeper who caused her much misery (665), and how she then had thrown him into the deep well. Moreover, she revealed to the king how the guardian outside of the castle [the servant], who had been the cause of the crime committed against her (670) by giving the evil advice and which had robbed her of her honor, had been hanged from a tree. Finally, she related to the king how she had talked with the maid (675) who had lain down with the king in her place on the first wedding night. Because she had pleaded with this nasty maid to leave the bed, to no avail (680), the latter had to die a miserable death through the painful fire at that time which she, the queen, had herself set (685). All this she revealed to her husband.

Once she was finished with her account, the king tenderly embraced his wife and drew her toward him, full of love: "You had to pay dearly for me," (690) he said to the lady. "I want to live with you forever as your loyal servant because you have suffered much on my behalf, there is no doubt about it (695). Neither your honor nor my appreciation of you will ever be diminished through any penance, either privately or publicly, because of this story." This was the good man's pledge upon his honor (700) to the lady.

According to my opinion, the noble king acted properly because the lady never did anything evil and yet fell into great sorrow (705) without guilt and intention [on her part]. But those who had stolen her honor had to pay dearly for it because each of them had to forfeit his life (710). It was only justice what happened to the knight's servant because of his evil advice: he was hanged like a common thief. He gave advice to his lord which was wrong and based on a lie (715). For this he was hanged from a branch. The knight also had to suffer punishment because of his enormously evil deed that he committed against the queen, when he badly deceived her with his words (720) and robbed her of her honor. For this reason she cut the head off his beautiful body. The gatekeeper also received his proper punishment from the queen (725) and so lost his life when he drowned in the well, after he had abused her noble body against her own will when he had forced her to be his woman [i.e., wife] (730). It was also justice what happened to the maid when she burned to ashes through the force of the fire, because she had wanted to have the king as her husband and stay with him forever (735). For this she received bad payment, which pleases me because she was full of disloyalty. All of them suffered the right penalty.

I would enjoy it (740) if the same were to happen to those of whom one knows, without any doubt and truly, that they lead a life of evil and filled with untrustworthiness (745). Truly, it makes me happy and seems to me to be good and proper when disloyalty strikes its originator, as happened to those four people. Nevertheless, the lady, so free of any cunning (750)—I mean the queen—had to suffer great misery. Because there was no evil in her, instead only goodness, (755) God granted her His mercy. He rescued her from all dangers. Repeatedly she would have died from her suffering if God had not assisted her. He does so for all those (760) who fall into danger without any fault of their own.

Herewith the tale, told to you by Kaufringer, comes to its conclusion.

No. 18
Anonymous: The Nightingale

The fourth tale told on the fifth day in Boccaccio's *Decameron* contains the same motif as the present *mære*, which is contained in the Bremen manuscript, Staatsbibliothek, Ms. b 42b, folios 164v-169v. The manuscript was written sometime in the early fifteenth century, but we do not know whether the German poet of our tale (*Nachtigall* [*Nightingale*] *A*) borrowed his material from Boccaccio (after 1350), or whether he drew it from other, older sources. The motif of 'catching the nightingale' with its strongly sexual connotation was widely disseminated in the Middle Ages; see, for instance, the *lai* "Laustic" by Marie de France (ca. 1170–1180). A considerable variation of our *mære* (*Nachtigall* [*Nightingale*] *B*) appeared in a Weimar manuscript (Zentralbibliothek der deutschen Klassik, Hs. O 145, compiled after 1480, but before 1490). That version seems to have been composed in Augsburg and is characterized by a slightly social-critical approach.

EDITION

Friedrich Heinrich von der Hagen, *Gesammtabenteuer*, 2: 71–82.

TEXT

Whenever a courtly, educated man knows of a curious report or of particularly unusual events, he should relate them to us. If one person among the audience does not like it (5), then another will enjoy hearing it if it is sensational enough. For this reason one should not keep such stories a secret. For this reason I cannot help telling you one (10).

As I heard, once there was a renowned knight who had his castle on a hill not far outside of the city, which was built very sturdily (15). It was just perfect. He himself owned many riches and had a beautiful daughter, but no other children, as I was told (20). She was beautiful and nicely shaped. One could not find any other maid or woman in the area or anywhere else in the country who could match her beauty. Nearby there was a courageous knight (25) who also possessed much wealth and was well positioned. He had an attractive son, and no other children

(30). He raised him well until he reached the age when he started to think of marrying. He was beautiful and intelligent (35), and made a good impression. He was not more than twenty years old. So both these two young people were in a perfect condition [to marry], and the young man made efforts (40) to woo the young woman for her love. He ruminated intensively on how to go about achieving his goal, as many young people do who eventually succeed in fulfilling their desire (45). This way he courted the maid all the time, hoping that she would grant him her favor and that he would be so fortunate. This young woman (50) was also favorably inclined toward him and would not have accepted either silver or gold in place of his love, however she might be able to find her way to him.

But the maid was kept so protected (55) in her father's house that no person could come near her, neither by day nor by night, neither within the house nor outside. This situation was great misfortune for the two young people (60).

In front of the house was an orchard surrounded by a strong hedge which protected it well. Flowers and grass grew inside the garden (65), and everything was nicely shaded by a large number of good trees covered with many green leaves. The noble knight had also planted many flowers and herbs (70) in his garden. People said, without lying, that the air in the garden was better and sweeter than anywhere else. To enter the garden (75) one had to go through a narrow door. The knight had built in front of the garden a high-vaulted pergola which served so that he could sit in that space (80) during the summer when he took his meal. He believed that it was more healthful to eat there.

One day the maid selected a messenger who was most fit for her intention, and sent him straight away (85) to the young man to let him know that he should be ready at night for everything to come and that he should arrive at the orchard (90) without being seen by anyone. There she wanted to wait for him. And if she could arrange matters properly she would be happy to fulfill his wishes (95). The young man was very pleased when he received the message the maid had sent him. His heart filled with joy, and he sent his thanks back to the young woman (100), thanking her for granting him so much love, and assuring her that he would be able to meet her at the specific spot.

When she had received his answer, she lay down on a bed and began to lament loudly (105). Her mother got very worried when she heard it, and came running to her daughter. She asked her: "Tell me, my little daughter, what has happened to you? (110) What might be the cause of your discomfort?" The daughter responded to her mother: "I have such a headache, which makes me very weak." When her father heard the news (115), he rushed to his daughter and asked: "Where does it hurt the most?" She answered: "Near the heart and elsewhere." He said: "Let us apply a good salve (120) that will take away your pain and your discomfort." The maid answered: "Father, I have found a better method (125) that will help me indeed if nothing else will be of use, which might easily be the case." He said:

"Daughter, don't keep it from me (130): whatever you wish will not be denied to you." She said: "Listen, I would like to sleep in the pergola in front of the orchard tonight because the sweet air in there, rising from the good herbs, (135) will ease my pain. And I would like to see whether a bird will come flying over from the orchard: perhaps I might catch it (140), and then I would be totally well again." "May God send you this bird!" said her mother in reply.

The parents ordered that soft and delightful bedding be spread outside (145) without any delay. They also put there something to eat and drink, and then the time to sleep had come. They forbade all servants to make any noise, (150) to allow the child not to be frightened or disturbed. Before it got totally dark, her mother came out to her one more time and asked her whether she needed anything else (155). The young woman said: "Mother, I need a glass of good wine, and please put it next to my bed so I can enjoy it later." (160) The wine was brought to her immediately, and then the mother locked the door behind her and left the daughter alone, who felt better there than anywhere else.

As soon as night had set in (165), the young man came sneaking to her, and since he was very skillful, he managed to find his way through the hedge. He brought a stick with him that he leaned against the hedge (170), which allowed him to climb over, and so he met the maid. They embraced each other full of love, and then went to bed, where they enjoyed the game of love (175) and had a wonderful time. They did not pay attention to the birds' singing. The night did not seem long to them, and, as I heard, when dawn began to break (180), they were still lying on the bed in tight embrace, tightly holding on to each other with their white arms.

The young woman said: "I have never experienced more happiness than tonight (185) when I held you in my arms, just as I wanted it." But then they both overslept until the sun rose. The young woman's mother felt a strong urge to see her and said to her husband (190): "It would frighten me if I cannot see the child right away. May God be merciful and let her still be alive."

He said: "Stay here (195), let me go myself." He put on his clothes, got up, and went to a little window to look out, to catch sight of his daughter (200), checking to see whether she found rest after her illness. But when he appeared out of the window, he saw the young man and his daughter lying together (205), resting peacefully together. He stood there and gazed at them carefully. They looked lovely while asleep. The bed coverings and their clothing (210) had slipped off them. The girl held his thing in her hand which was standing upright in all its force and stretched out like a lance and was proudly erect in front of her (215).

The knight did not go into the pergola because he had seen them sleeping together. Instead he returned to his bed and said: "My dear wife, get up and take a look (220): your daughter has done well; she has caught the bird, as she said she wanted to do last night, and is holding it by its neck." She answered: "You are making fun of me!" (225) He said: "Oh no, wife, by God, you better believe me that, it has a head of brilliant colors and could not be more beautiful." "Oh dear, that poor bird!" (230), she said, "now I also must go and find out the truth."

She went to the window and looked down where the young man and the maid were lying together (235) and resting peacefully. When the mother discovered them, she tore her hair and screamed: "Why had my mother ever carried me as a baby!" [expression of desperation] She wrung her hands together (240).

At that moment the young man woke up and heard the loud noise and noticed that the sun was shining brightly. He called out: "Oh dear, Lord, oh dear! We have slept too long here on this bed." (245)

Now the knight came through the door and said to the maid: "Daughter, have you caught the bird? Have you recovered? I think this is all good. Your catch gives us much to think about (250). Now take good care of the bird, so that it won't escape from you again."

The young man said: "Dear sir, let this not be harmful to me, please." The knight answered: "This will not hurt you at all, (255) if you take her as your wife. Since you both have slept with each other, take the next step and join in earnest."

The young man said: "I would love to marry her."

So he became her husband (260). Both fathers gave them many goods and made them rich. They were happy and enjoyed public esteem and honor. That is all I have to say about the nightingale.

No. 19
Hans Rosenplüt (?): The Painter (Woodcarver) in Würzburg

The Nuremberg craftsman poet Hans Rosenplüt (ca. 1426–1460) enjoyed considerable popularity for his rhymed narratives and Shrovetide plays, but we cannot be certain that the present tale was also composed by him, although it has been recorded in six manuscripts along with other tales that are unmistakably attributed to Rosenplüt (even by name). However, none of the six manuscripts from ca. 1460 until ca. 1524–1526 specifically identifies the present author, whereas Rosenplüt usually added his name in the last lines of his works. *Of the Painter in Würzburg* is based on a earlier version, the *Herrgottschnitzer* (thirteenth century, *The Carver of Crucifixes*), but the author replaced some of the rather shockingly blasphemous elements with harmless, though still titillating details. Instead of pretending to be the figure on a crucifix, the priest here acts the role of a wooden saint's figure. In the older tale the narrator had also emphasized that the painting of the priest's body was to be seen in parallel to the Jews' treatment of Christ's body, which Rosenplüt (?) leaves out entirely, focusing instead exclusively on the erotic entertainment.

EDITION

Klaus Grubmüller, ed., *Novellistik des Mittelalters*, 928–34.

TEXT

Would you now please be quiet and listen, since I would like to tell you of an extraordinary adventure concerning a smart man who experienced many unusual things. He lived in Würzburg. Whatever was able to fly or could move (5), he knew how to paint or to carve in some material. He knew many arts and was able to do many different things. He was married to the most beautiful woman (10); no other woman could be found who would have been her equal. The vicar of the cathedral was enamored of her and often wooed her in secret, begging her to let him come in between her knees.

One day she wanted to go to mass (15) when the vicar approached her, greeted her lovingly, and said: "Lady, I would make you rich if I were allowed to lie with you for one night; and if I knew for certain that it would remain a secret (20) I would give you sixty measures of silver and a coat and a dress." The woman answered: "Wait until tomorrow morning, then come back here and I will let you know my decision, (25) whether I can do it despite my husband."

The woman quickly ran home and called her husband to her. She said: "Do you know the vicar of the cathedral? He has whispered into my ear (30) that he would give me sixty measures of silver and also would buy me a coat and a dress if I let him lie with me for one night. Now, give me your advice (35) as to how we can deceive him. It seems to be best if you [pretend] to go on a journey, since then we will get the money from him, and then you come back by surprise. In the meantime I will let him come to me. We cannot come up with a better plan to cheat him out of his money." (40)

The man said: "If we can deceive this jerk in the bed here at home, so that the stupid fool would get terribly frightened in this adventure with us, it would give us a good profit (45). Tell him already today to come to our house." The painter left his house and went away.

Soon thereafter she sent her chambermaid to the vicar, asking him to come before he sat down to dinner, and also not to forget the money (50). The vicar soon came running to her. She said: "Give me the money and pour it into my lap, then I will pay you back with much joy."

When he had handed over the money (55), she put a chicken on a skewer and placed it over the fire. Then they both sat down at the table and ate and drank and enjoyed life. The vicar was so overjoyed (60) that he served the woman himself.

Then the husband knocked at the door. The wife screamed: "My husband is coming home!" The vicar asked her: "How do we manage it so I can save my life?" (65) She answered: "I will give you good advice: strip off all your clothing, then I will paint you yellow and red and apply the colors white and blue. Then you stand among the wooden figures (70) and hide among them, leaning against the wall, and then my husband will not recognize you." The vicar stripped and even took off his underpants.

Meanwhile the painter uttered many curses because she did not let him in (75). She, however, painted the vicar in all these colors and put him in the row of figures. Then she ran to the house door and removed the bolt. When the husband came in (80), he said: "Wife, give me a light. I am coming from a customer who says he would like to buy a sculpture. Let me look and see whether I have one for him." The wife quickly brought him a light (85) with which he looked at the wall. There he noticed the vicar's head and hair. He said: "For sure, indeed, the journeyman who created this figure must truly sit at the head of our table with all honors

(90). This figure is executed as well as if it were alive. I must give the journeyman a better weekly salary."

Then he looked more carefully further down and said: "Wife, what is that?" He looked at the vicar's genitals (95). "Wife, why is it hanging down so untidily? Give me a little ax and let me chop it off, since it seems to be an offense to women." The wife said: "No, my dear husband, women put their wax candles on it." (100) Nevertheless she handed him a little ax.

The vicar got scared and turned pale; he rushed along the wall and went back and forth, pushing down almost twelve statues. He struggled toward the door (105). The painter ran behind him and screamed: "Break down the bridges and block the streets! All my sculptured figures are running away from me. One is escaping from me as fast as an arrow. It was truly made out of the best ash wood (110) I had found in the forest. My journeyman carved it with his own hands."

The vicar reached his home and was entirely out of breath. Outside the house the painter made a loud commotion and banged on the door (115). The vicar yelled from above: "Who is there?" The painter replied: "Sir, listen to this amazing story. I am a poor painter. One of my sculptures has run away. I had intended to sell it to-morrow (120). I would have easily gotten a hundred pounds for it." The vicar said: "Keep your mouth shut; look at [what I am giving you] and take it away with you, but make sure that no one notices anything."

The painter became a very happy man (125) and carried the hundred pounds with him and brought them home to his wife. He let her see them and then put them into her lap. The wife preserved her honor (130), and the painter was also an honorable person. I cannot tell you anything else of these two. This story is now coming to its end. If anyone were to give me some wine, I would drink and gulp it down until tears flowed out of my eyes.

No. 20
COUNT FROBEN CHRISTOPH VON ZIMMERN: THE DISAPPOINTED LOVER

One of the earliest instances of the German reception of Boccaccio's *Decameron* can be found in the voluminous *Zimmerische Chronik* (Chronicle of the Lord of Zimmern) by Count Froben Christoph von Zimmern (1519-1566). He based it on the personal notes and various texts written by his uncle, the historian and collector Baron Wilhelm Wernher (or Werner) von Zimmern (1485-1575). Froben worked on compiling this fascinating family chronicle from 1558/1559 until his death, without ever managing to complete his work. His uncle Wilhelm Wernher von Zimmern had studied at the universities of Freiburg, Vienna, and Bologna and had developed into a highly cultivated and learned person with great interests both in classical literature from antiquity and the Middle Ages, and in history. He was certainly an expert in astronomy, mathematics, and geometry; he spoke Italian well, and was particularly educated in law. We know that he translated various texts by Latin authors into German. His contemporaries regarded him as an accomplished and highly skillful diplomat and jurist who held a position at the imperial court of justice in Speyer. Apart from extensive collections of coins, artifacts, medallions, bones, horns, stones, etc.—his so-called *Wunderkammer* (Chamber of Miraculous Things)—he assembled many different texts about his family history and published numerous chronicles of other noble Swabian families, especially a chronicle of the archishopric of Mainz, but he also wrote a most fascinating *mære*, "Der enttäuschte Liebhaber," or *The Disappointed Lover*. It is in part based on the seventh tale on the sixth day in Boccaccio's *Decameron* (ca. 1350), which von Zimmern must have read in its first German translation by Arigo (a pseudonym for Heinrich Schlüsselfelder), which was printed in 1472 or 1473 in Ulm. But contrary to scholarly opinions,[1] the similarities are not so

---

[1] See Hanns Fischer, *Die deutsche Märendichtung des 15. Jahrhunderts*, Münchener Texte und Untersuchungen zur deutschen Literatur des Mittelalters 12 (Munich: Beck, 1966); idem, *Studien zur deutschen Märendichtung* (Tübingen: Niemeyer, 1968), 2nd rev. and expanded ed. prepared by Johannes Janota (Tübingen: Niemeyer, 1983); and Ursula Kocher, *Boccaccio und die deutsche Novellistik: Formen der Transposition italienischer 'novelle' im 15. und 16. Jahrhundert*, Chloe: Beihefte zum Daphnis 38 (Amsterdam and New York: Editions Rodopi, 2005).

close, and the German author can really be credited with having created his own original tale, if we disregard the metadiegetic account[2] within the tale about the courageous lady of Prato who defended herself successfully against an iron law imposed by the patriarchal city government on the female population. Von Zimmern seems to have been familiar with other verse narratives, but he copied down only this one example, which his nephew later incorporated into his chronicle.[3] The handwritten copy of Count Froben Christoph von Zimmern's *Chronik,* in two volumes, is today housed in Stuttgart, Württembergische Landesbibliothek, Cod. Donaueschingen 580 and 581. In the prose introduction to his tale, Froben Christoph von Zimmern claims that his account is based on Johannes Wernher von Zimmern's personal experience, which modern scholarship, however, has mostly discredited. But it is important to know that Wernher had dedicated his text to Duke Eberhart of Württemberg.

Here as in all other cases I am rendering the verse text into prose. The verse count in Barack's edition is typical for his time, but it does not conform to modern practice, since he counts the verses anew every page (1-45, 49, 51, or 54, etc.), instead of providing us with a complete verse count of the entire narrative (as Fischer does in his anthology *Die deutsche Märendichtung* [Munich: Beck, 1966]). In order to facilitate the identification of specific passages, I am providing page counts in bold once every time before the first line, and then follow Barack's verse count for every five lines.

EDITION

Zimmerische Chronik, ed. Karl August Barack, 2nd ed., 4 vols. (Freiburg i. Br. and Tübingen: J. C. B. Mohr, 1881), 1; see also the digitized version at: http://de.wikisource.org/wiki/Zimmerische_Chronik#Projektfortschritt. For a modern edition, though deliberately shortened, leaving out especially the paralipomena (supplementary texts), including our *mære,* see *Die Chronik der Grafen von Zimmern,* ed. Hansmartin Decker-Hauff and Rudolf Seigel, 3 vols (Constance and Stuttgart: Jan Thorbecke, 1964–1972) (incomplete).

---

[2] This is a technical term for stories told by a character inside a diegetic narrative. 'Diegetic' means, according to Gérard Genette (*Figures I–III;* 1967-1970), who coined the term, the primary story. 'Extradiegetic' means the story that frames the primary story (see: http://www.cla.purdue.edu/english/theory/narratology/terms/narrativetermsmainframe.html; last accessed on August 27, 2006).

[3] It is difficult to find relevant information on this tale, but see Hanns Fischer, *Studien zur deutschen Märendichtung,* 2nd ed. (Tübingen: Niemeyer, 1983), 188–89; Ursula Kocher, *Boccaccio und die deutsche Novellistik* (Amsterdam and New York: Editions Rodopi, 2005), 289–329. The best introduction to Count Froben Christoph of Zimmern can be found in Beat Rudolf Jenny, *Graf Froben Christoph von Zimmern* (Lindau and Constance: J. Thorbecke, 1959). Now see also Erica Bastress-Dukehart, *The Zimmern Chronicle* (Aldershot, England, and Burlington, VT: Ashgate, 2002).

TEXT

[586] It happened in a city not far away from Aachen [west of Cologne] that one evening I was going for a walk in the street. I thought: "It is still early" (40), so I stood still and looked around to see what beautiful young women there might be, such as maids, wives, and also young girls, all beautifully built and attractive. There was a throng of lay people and clerics (45) [587] standing around in a ring. When the dance began, I saw one row of dancers, maybe two, approaching me and moving away, and at the end I noticed (5) a young maid with brown hair whom I immediately fell in love with. I knew not this or that, whether I should hold one thing or let it go. The reason was that I burned with love (10) for this maid. I thought: "My God, any person would immediately get well who would gain this fruit. Whatever hurtful experience he might have resulting from this love, he would regard with disdain." (15) I saw that the maid was always alone. And as I was looking at her, I got up and approached her. When I came near to her, she asked me to sit down next to her (20) and greeted me with polite [intelligent] words as was most appropriate. She looked sweetly at me. My heart filled with more and more flames, so much that I suddenly (25) could not utter a word because of overpowering love. She realized this quickly, though she was still a child in age, but she was not blind to it (30). She said: "Young man, take courage! Your hopes still might come true. I observe that you have lost your head because of a love that is not being reciprocated to you. I beg you, tell me the truth (35), maybe I can give you advice which might take you to your goal. Tomorrow will be another day. What cannot be today, might be achievable tomorrow! Let your sorrow go! (40) I recognize a loyal person in you, therefore I hope that much good will be granted to you."

I thanked her right away; her words had opened my [locked] lips, and I was freed from the bond (45). So I began to talk and openly told her what was on my mind, that she held me captive and that I wondered whether she would grant me her mercy [588] and give me her love and loyalty. I spoke about my feelings with many words which she fully comprehended. Laughingly she looked at me and said to me, poking fun at me (5): "Fellow, do you take me for such a person as would immediately open her door to such a strange man of whom I know nothing? I guess you come from the land of monkeys (10); I tell you honestly that you are not educated enough about the proper path that pertains to these things."

Then she spoke further: "You are a foolish man to seek friendship (15) with a strange woman so quickly and to ask for her hand [literally: body]. I think the wine has done this to you, or perhaps the moon has confused your brain."

I responded: "Lady, do not be angry with me! (20) Listen one more time to my pleading and do not display your anger! I was only joking when I spoke to you and asked you for your love." (25)

I hoped to have amended the situation thereby, but I caused even more damage. I thought that she intended to hit me. Only now did she begin to complain bitter, saying that I was the kind of boy (30) who would behave most impolitely against her. She said: "Did you read it anywhere in books that one should seduce women that way? Damn, what a shame! One should not allow you to stay here in this country (35). What disgrace that you are still here [idiomatic phrase that cannot be fully translated] and that you are twisting all honor. You are a crazy man, and this will not be of any help to you."

Then she turned away from me, saying (40): "I would truly be pleased if you were gone." Great fear made me feel hot and cold; her words were extremely hurtful and I did not know what I had done wrong to ruin everything so badly (45). I had no idea what to say to her. I said to myself: "The devil has brought me here. If I contradict her [589] and repeat what I said before, she might really blame me for being a man without virtues and would say that I had a licentious mind. I do not know whether it would help at all [to reply to her]."

As I was sitting there, ruminating (5), she said: "Lazy fool, how low do you intend to let your head bow down to the ground? Wait a little, let the night arrive! I see well that you desire wine which you can see in front of your eyes." (10)

She spoke these and many other mocking words. I thought to myself: "No, you had better get out of here quietly as long as the case is as it is! You cannot achieve anything better now."

I got up and left (15), whereas the dance continued as usual. I placed myself behind the other dancers, weighed down with sorrow. My mind was filled with many contradictory thoughts. One time I got the idea: "God might suddenly help you (20), and then she might think well of you." But immediately my mind changed: "Gosh, what made you believe that you might transform her feelings [literally: voice] toward one who is not in her heart? (25) What a fool you are to forget the words that she spoke? Go home, lie down on your bed! You will profit much more from that. You can clearly see that she does not care for you (30) and has little feelings for you [literally: has little love pangs because of you]."

Only now my hair began to stand on end up toward heaven, and my blood started to curdle so that I could hardly hold back my tears (35). I had to lean on a wall because I could no longer stand. I thought: "What a man burdened with sorrow and struggle I am right now because a woman has put me so tightly in bonds!" (40)

I tortured myself over this matter which occupied me entirely. I thought I would lose my life if I could not win her love. While I was meditating all this (45), the dance came to an end, so I decided to look and see where the maid would go. She went with other women. [590] I closely watched her. When she reached a stone gate she encountered a young monk in a grey habit. I do not know what he said to her (5), but she paid close attention to his words. Then both kissed each other passionately [literally: she threw her lips toward him, and both kissed]. With how much pain I was filled [at that sight] anyone can judge for himself (10) who has ever felt love in his heart. I stood there like an imbecile without moving. I knew that this was her own wish. I was dumbfounded that I had lost them out of sight (15). I had no idea where they had gone. In all my life I have never felt the time passing so slowly. Finally they appeared again, but I did not know at all from where (20), whether from the cellar, or from another room where they had sat down. I cannot remember.

At that moment an old man came out of the house, (25) who had clearly seen them kissing each other. Where he then had gone, or what he had heard or learned about these two, I do not know (30) because the sun gave me headaches. When the old man saw the maid—do you want to hear what he said?—: "Woman, where have you been? Did you pick up everything (35) that had been lying here on the street crookedly? [idiomatic phrase] If I were to begin a fight with you here I would profit very little from it. I will wait until we get home."

When I heard those words (40)—I do not know where the monk had disappeared to—the young woman went off. I followed her up to the door that she entered. Next to it was my inn (45) where I was staying. That made me feel so much better, knowing that I lived next door to her, although I was distraught, [591] as you have heard before, about the loss of her love. I quickly ran up the stairs and thought myself whether I might manage (5) to watch the couple or listen to their words. I looked all over the wall to see whether I could find a little hole. Finally I detected (10) a crack in the wall. I put my head to it and sat down because I wanted to look whether I might not be able to see the woman who had been so attractive to me (15). While I was gazing through the crack, I espied my beloved; immediately my love-pangs were gone because I could again see her whom I had met that day (20), except that the monk then had stepped into my garden [idiomatic phrase = love territory], although I had not asked him at all to do so. I had requited him very little for being in love with the one whom I loved with my whole heart (25). I would not have believed that of her after the words she had uttered to me. Afterwards I had grabbed my hiking stick and had walked away, as I have said before (30).

I pressed my eye to the wall and wanted to observe everything that was going to happen on the other side between the young woman and the old man. Now the time had progressed so much (35) that darkness had set in because of the night, and I could not see well through the crack. I do not know what she thought, but soon the chambermaid came in with a little light (40) and stuck it up on the wall. There was also a screen, so I could not see her when she went to bed. As soon as she had changed her clothes, she lay down (45). At that moment the old man entered the room, foaming at the mouth like a wild boar, bent on starting a big fight. [592] First he closed the door. He lay down on the bed with his clothes on as if he suffered from a major illness. Then he looked at the young woman. Would you like to hear what he said? (5)

"You know well, my darling, what you have done. What shall I give you as your reward? I have often enough forbidden you to see the monk and I have often beaten you, but it has not helped a bit (10). Tomorrow will be the fourth day that I am going to punish you for it. I have also implored you and tried to employ kindness in my treatment of you. But nothing has been of any use (15); you are not abandoning your old cunning, you are the monk's slave."

The young woman turned around, acting as if she had been deeply asleep, and said to the old man (20): "You have lied to me, and if you were willing to tell the truth, then you have seen me sitting on the monk and not the monk on me, and you can believe me that." (25) Then she turned her back to him, keeping quiet as if she were a mute. Only now did I see the man in most horrible shape. His heart was burning with fury. He uttered many curses against the woman (30) who did not care about it at all, never mind how loud he swore and yelled, and kept pretending as if she were sleeping. He [on the other hand] screamed so much I can repeat only some of his words (35), otherwise it would take too long. But then his love for his wife and his wrath mingled. Since he thought she was asleep (40), he began to tear his hair and said: "O eternal God, what disgrace and mockery it is for me that I have to look at this shamefulness! She will no longer get (45) all the food that I used to let her have. And if I have to apply the sifter, she will not get more than just a little dust. Oh, why am I so deaf? [593] Since there is no other way today, see, an animal goes where it finds its food. I cannot be angry with her because she fills all my heart. Rather than separating from her (5), I will avoid her."

He said many more words, and midnight was approaching. He needed to go to sleep. His anger had abated (10). The young woman, however, had a different plan. As soon as he had fallen asleep, she turned to him quickly and screamed out loud. She yelled: "You, my beloved treasure (15), you have done a deadly deed to me by not coming to bed at night. You have terribly frightened me."

The old man abruptly woke up and yelled: "Damn you, you cursed bag! (20) Why did you not scream like that when the monk enjoyed you in the straw and fulfilled his lust with you in a dark corner? One day you will rot (25) and maybe even die!"

The young woman replied to the old man, whom she saw lying in bed: "Oh, my dear husband, you have truly done injustice to me (30). You did not see me doing that. You must have dreamed it. I have never had any other man but you, which you can fully believe of me. If I knew that you mean it in earnest [that you want to leave me] (35), and that you truly believe what you charged me with, I would not wait until tomorrow morning and would never lie down with you again."

Herewith she put her head down on the pillow and cried bitter tears (40). She also wrung her hands. "No person will ever find me with another man, God willing," said the young woman to her old husband.

Again the old man began to speak (45): "I have never seen a more deceptive woman who intends to put me to shame with her words and blind me when I have open eyes. You know that when I came here last night I was so furious (50) and punished you [594] for what I witnessed. And now you want to deceive me with words. I demonstrate the truth of my words: when I told you that I saw how the monk gave you his blessing and how he was lying on top of you (5), you immediately replied and argued against it (I still have not yet forgotten it), claiming that you had been sitting on the monk, and not the monk on you (10). Moreover, you claimed that you had lain with a Franciscan monk, when in reality it was a Dominican. You use such false words with me, so you had better be quiet!" (15)

Only now did true sorrow and pain set in. The young woman turned away and began to cry and to lament, speaking the following words, as I am going to repeat to you: "Oh dear, oh dear, poor me (20), may God have pity on me. I am suffering such injustice from this really evil creature! When he overloads himself with wine, he loses his mind [literally: voice] (25), as now has happened. At night you could not see much, and you could hardly walk or stand upright without the help of a stick. The proof for that is obvious (30): you are still lying there like a pig. You cannot escape from this truth because you could not even undress. When I intended to pull you down into bed, you responded with cussing (35) and with so much reprimanding that I, poor woman, had to suffer much. When you dream of something, as has happened tonight, when your mind is sodden with wine (40), then you always want to evaluate everything as evil, and you do nothing but scream and yell in an absurd manner. The truth is not hidden from me: you are still lying there (45) and smell like a barrel of vinegar. I am saying this, whether it will help me or hurt me. May God help me that the day will begin soon so that I can leave! [595] I would rather drown myself or hang myself with a rope than to suffer this any longer. I would fare better in Hell than in this life filled with strife (5). I swear that this is the truth."

Then her whole body began to shake as if she were filled with a fever, and she rolled her eyes. I am telling you honestly (10), she acted as if she were dead. I would lose all inclination to laugh if I had to see a man in such shape, not to speak of a woman, and would rather forgo such an experience (15) and look for other entertainment.

The old man got really frightened when the girl was lying there like this. There were two reasons for it: his fear and his love for her (20). He was convinced of what he saw her doing before his eyes, and he believed that her illness was his fault. He decided to lift her up and put her on the bed. He loved her so much (25) that he would not have taken any amount of money from a duke as payment for her and to lose her that way. When she slowly recovered, he took her hand in his (30) and said to her: "If you are willing to believe me, then I will swear upon my oath that I deeply regret what has happened to you (35), especially your illness."

The young woman then said in a weak voice, when she looked at the old man: "If I have not yet suffered enough because of your intention to mock me (40), on top of my suffering and pain that I feel in my heart and that you impose on me, then my life will come to an end." With these words she fell back onto the pillow as if her last minute had arrived. When the grey-haired man saw it, he screamed out loud: "Murder, do I have to lose her? I do not want to live any longer (50) because I will become nothing [596] if she dies."

These words and many others the old man uttered out of great sorrow. "Oh God, let it happen that I will see her healthy again (5)! For the rest of my life I will give you a regular donation. Also, Saint James, dear lord, help me. I will also give you a gift (10): free me of this worry!"

As soon as he had promised this, the young woman opened an eye as if she had recovered somewhat (15). When the old man saw this, he felt much better in his heart. He lifted his hands up toward God and said: "O, gracious Lord, You rule through Your Law. He who trusts You (20) will be helped, as was the case with me. I will give thanks to You for the rest of my life!"

Then he turned to his wife: "Oh, my heart-beloved (25), I must say truthfully, a great sign has been given today through you, and for this reason we should rightly honor God (30) and increase His praise."

Now, my lords, notice what happened. The young woman spoke to the old man: "I should have died: then Saint James (35) would have given me [eternal] life. I am still suffering from the pain that you have caused me. All this was not enough for you and you continue to make fun of me (40). God will not let this go unpunished, and you will receive your reward for it because you did injustice to me in what you accused me of."

Then the old man knelt down [literally: bowed] (45) in front of the young woman and said: "I beg you, understand my words correctly! You must be truly aware that I will make every effort [597] to give you honor and property and compensate for your suffering. After all, I can fully understand that I acted wrongly against you. It will not happen to you again (5), when I will be drunk with wine. If I imagine such things once again, attribute this to my foolishness! Therefore I promise you that you will be free of all punishment from me!" (10) Then he gave her a jewel as a gift, which made the young woman very happy.

[He said further:] "I will pledge one more thing: you can live as it pleases you and be your own mistress (15), which I promise you as compensation for the suffering and the injustice that I committed against you!"

Thereupon the young woman simply said: "Because you have let me unjustly feel (20) your wrath so often, this has shortened my life and I will have to die early. But part of the penance is that one forgives the deed (25) which another has committed. Consequently, insofar as you identified your own guilt and confessed that you were in the wrong, bend down, I want to forgive you (30) and accept your promise that you will never do it again."

The grey-haired man answered: "Heart-beloved, I implore you not to think of the past any more (35), and then I will hand over the key to everything that I own, which then all will be your property."

Then he took her into his arms. This fills an old man with cold and heat (40), and also makes a child out of a man, and blinds a man with open eyes. After all, he thought that her intentions were honest, and he had completely forgotten (45) what had filled his heart before, such as the disgrace he had experienced but which had now disappeared from his mind. Herewith their fight was settled [598] and all strife completely resolved.

The old man lay down next to the young woman. His previous sorrow was entirely compensated through the rich love, whereas this love left the young woman quite cold (5), although she acted the same way as he did and as if she felt the need to thank God. The old man continued to be a sour apple in her mouth, but she did not let him notice it (10). Only sometimes the old man caught a glimpse [of the truth] with his eyes. Otherwise she knew how to manipulate her old husband well and make him believe everything she said (15).

Since she had managed to control him entirely, listen to what he did. She spoke the following words: "My most heart-beloved husband, I would like to reveal to you (20), if it does not irritate you, that it is entirely for nought if a man is afraid of his wife, as the old proverb says, which you have heard often (25): A woman's best protection is what she does herself, because when a woman does not safeguard her honor, neither little nor big things can be of help. Let me tell you further (30) what once happened a long time ago.

[Here begins the story directly borrowed from Boccaccio]

In the noble city of Prato [near Florence] they once had a law that any woman, if she committed adultery, would forfeit her life (35), and nothing could rescue her: she would be burned at the stake, against which there was no help. The same penalty applied (40) to those who took money for sex or who attacked religion. In this city it happened one day that a young noble lady, called the beautiful Philippa (45), was caught by her husband, called Rinaldo, [599] with a young man in her bedroom. The latter was also of noble family and was called Lazarino. He had slept with the beautiful lady, who loved him as much as she loved herself (5). They had their arms and legs intertwined; I believe that they both had done what they had desired. When her husband discovered them, great sorrow resulted from this (10). He almost lost his mind and hardly would have hesitated to kill them both. He was prevented from this only because he was afraid of the young man (15), which caused mixed feelings in him and softened his wrath somewhat, though he could not control himself entirely. He immediately thought of the aforementioned law and ruling (20). He called together his housemaids and servants and many other people, asking them to come to him. He let them all see the young man lying with the lady (25), so that in case he needed it he would have witnesses. As soon as the day began, the husband led his wife to the court of justice. When the lady arrived there (30), she collected herself well, undaunted by facing either good or evil. She controlled herself well, as is the habit of women who have a lover (35). She looked up smilingly and asked her friends to come to her support. She asked them for advice on how to defend herself, how to avoid being shamed (40) and then burned at the stake.

Her friends made loud noise [in their deliberations] and suggested she consider running away and escaping from the court of justice and hiding far away (45). But she did not like any of these ideas, since they did not appeal to her. For a good while she stood by herself, and then she acted in the way of those who excel through strong character. She consulted with herself for a while (50) and distanced herself from all their counsel [600] because she wanted to fight for her right, whether it would bring her harm or success. She wanted to die with a strong character rather than to fail in life with a deceptive result. She had no intention of not acknowledging the man (5) in whose arms she had slept. Once she had considered all this, she quickly went up to the judge. When she had reached that point before him, she displayed a free, friendly character (10) and asked the judge what her husband accused her of. The judge was a virtuous, honest man. He began to speak and told her what her husband accused her of (15), that is, that he had found the young man in the [marital] bed sleeping in her arms. For that reason he [the judge] had to punish her according to the city laws and statutes, 'unless [as he said] you deny the accusation (20), whereas your husband blames you for this deed. Consider how you might want to defend yourself!'

The lady looked at the judge without any fear; then she spoke to him in a well-mannered fashion, humbly and charmingly: 'Sir Judge, I do not deny the deed (25): I was sleeping with Lazerino [sic], happily enjoying this love. I will never say that I regret what I did because I do not know any other man in this world (30) whom I love more. This love is growing from day to day. But listen to what else I have to say: Sir Judge, you ought to know that all laws, statutes, and rules (35) should be equal for all, whether they are great or small, and apply to all, both to the poor and to the rich (40), both to women and to men. It would not be proper or be a good statute which would concern only women, but not men (45), making the former the only ones subject to the law. That would seem to me to be a mockery [of justice] and also contrary to God's will. You men have set up this statute **[601]** never thinking to include a woman in the deliberations. How can this be appropriate, that we women here on earth have to do penance but not you men? (5) Therefore I say openly that your statute is not right. Whatever you might want to do, you will condemn your soul to Hell because you are taking my life (10) and killing me. This is certainly in your power.

'But there is one more thing to consider, and if you are pleased to listen to it (15), grant me the time until I will have told you all.

'That is, ask my husband whether I have ever failed in obeying him (20). Whenever he desired me, I was always ready; how often and how many times he demanded it from me, I have never denied it to him." (25)

Thereupon the husband spoke up and said: 'Sir Judge, she is speaking the truth. There was never a time that I desired her and she refused me.'

As soon as the husband had made this statement (30), the wife reflected quickly and then turned to the judge again: 'Since my husband consequently always got his needs fulfilled, fully according to his heart's desire (35), where should I then have put the additional love which he could not use? Should I then have thrown it out to the dogs? Would it not have been better (40) to give it to a young nobleman and comply with his wishes insofar as he is asking me for my love, and especially to grant it to one who loves me more than himself (45)? It seems to me that it would be better to act in this way than to let this love get spoiled.'

There were many men and women in the audience who began to look at each other. **[602]** They had assembled at the outer ring of the court to observe how this case would develop.

Now, as the lady delivered her spirited, courageous speech right there and then and they all had heard her answer (5), everyone present called to the judge that the woman was right and had spoken properly in her short speech, and that her husband was in the wrong (10). They also shouted to the judge that the laws were too harsh, wherefore he should consider it appropriate to remove the one [specific] law, and declare it null and void (15), as it hurt women only. Only those should be punished who sold their bodies for money.

When all this happened and the husband realized (20) that he reaped only shame and mockery, he quickly left the court of justice. The beautiful woman stood there filled with joy, as people do until today who here on earth (25) are suddenly freed from the death [penalty]. Modestly she received the court's final judgment and returned home."

[Here ends the story borrowed from Boccaccio, and the original story continues]

The young woman then sat up and reflected a little while (30). Then she started to speak again and said to the old man: "Heart-beloved, let me ask you this: have you now understood me by way of what I just told you (35), and if so, then let me know how you liked it."

The old man turned to the young woman, acting as if he were asleep, and stayed quiet. After some minutes he began to speak because he had considered the matter closely (40), and addressed the young woman: "I will let everything stand as agreed upon and as I have promised you, and I will not retract anything."

This pleased the young woman very much (45), and with this the lord became the servant, as it is proper for old asses to suffer such a destiny. This is just right and fitting for those who hardly can find rest and yet run after any penny [idiomatic expression, hard to render] (50).

Now I let this be [603] and won't touch it any more, and won't ever talk about it again.

Meanwhile the dawn was coming, the time for us to rise. This forced me to leave my spot (5) so as to avoid anyone noticing what I had learned [through my spying]. Now listen to me what I am going to tell you. Time passed until noon, when I was sitting in front of the house (10), waiting to see whether the young woman would come out [to the street], hoping to speak with her and to beg her in a friendly manner and to reveal to her my suffering, sitting on the old grist [idiomatic phrase = which had not changed at all, since I still felt strong love] (15), just like Engeleier's servant [idiomatic expression, reference to an unknown satiric tale]. [I was hopeful] although the words available to me were still just simple and plain. But I was sitting there all alone and had mentally prepared myself well.

I was looking at the lady's door (20), when she came out of the house and approached me, asking why I was sitting there. [I answered:] "Oh, lady, if it might seem proper for you, and if you don't mind listening to me for a short while, then I will tell you what is my intention [literally: opinion] (25). I am sitting here only because of you. You can free me from my sorrow and make me happy, whatever you might order me to do; if I could serve you I would be completely liberated from all suffering (30). Now [I hope] you will clearly understand my true wishes."

She answered me: "You have come at a good time: I really need a servant who knows how to cut wood and ride horseback, and work in the meadow, whenever I might grant it to him (35).[4] Further, you must look out that you understand how to chop wood and how to do many other rough jobs which I do not all mention right now." With this she began to laugh (40). I was not sure whether she was serious

---

[4] Perhaps this might be a pornographic allusion, since these farm activities have often been used in poetic discourse for this purpose: see, for instance, the erotic songs by Oswald von Wolkenstein (1376/77-1445); for further examples, see Stefan Zeyen, . . . *daz tet der liebe dorn: Erotische Metaphorik in der deutschsprachigen Lyrik des 12.-14. Jahrhunderts* (Essen: Item-Verlag, 1996). But the young woman also implies a satirical rejection of his wooing, as the subsequent narrative development will indicate.

or fooling me. Also, she could not stay with me any longer without becoming the object of suspicions, so she left me (45).

I sat there as before, thinking deeply: "How this unpredictable situation is changing for this lady! I believe that a whole gang of charlatans [jesters?] [604] would not be a match for her. Oh, if only she would grant me her love! Then I would be so happy. My longing for her drives me crazy and robs me of all my strength (5) so that I cannot have one quiet minute day or night."

At that moment she returned and said to me: "Hey, my friend, one thing I want to tell you (10): I well understood you before, that you are trying to woo me with your words. Now I also feel the same way [love for you?]. I tell you how and where you must search for such a location [literally: strategy] (15) in the house where you can stay, that is, behind the fireplace, where you must wait for me. I will go into my house right away and come to you on the other side of the wall (20). There is an old dark hole. Even though you won't see me, you will be able to hear me."

Thereupon she left me and disappeared into her house. I also went away (25) and looked for the fireplace and sat down behind it. Never before or after did I experience a worse time, because the smoke hurt me badly (30). Had I committed the same sins as Nero had, I would have done my penance right there. I sat there until the evening. Often I thought: "Where is the hole, or when will she come here? (35) I believe that she has made me sit here simply out of vicious cunning. Oh God, let it happen that she will come to me!"

I already believed that it was all a sham (40), but at that moment she arrived and asked: "By God, how are you doing? It grieves me badly that I had to let you stay here alone. I was so busy (45) that I would not even have been able to spin one thread. My husband was here [all the time]. Only now has he left the house and will not return home today (50). Therefore I want to invite you in [605] to come to my bedroom. There I want to have you sit down and I will recompense you for your suffering, because I tell you openly that I have never loved anyone more [than you]." (5)

I said: "I would love to experience [literally: see] it, if only one thing could happen, that is, that you will no longer have any relationship with the monk or talk with him." (10)

She answered: "You, my highest treasure, I will pledge to you by my loyalty that I will never speak to him again in my whole life, neither just a few words or at length (15), and you can rest assured about that, upon my full fidelity! Go now for a short while, and then I will let you know through the maid whom I am going to send to you, (20) who will give you clear directions [literally: truth]. So leave now and wait for the maid!"

When she had finished she offered me her hand, extending it through the hole in the wall (25). I went to the dining room where the innkeeper had set the table getting ready for dinner. I sat down at the table as I was told to do, joining my fellows (30). The meal might have been chicken or fish, I did not pay any attention, the reason for which was the happiness that filled me.

But soon enough my mood changed. The table was removed, as is customary (35), and they brought in water [for hand-washing]. At the door I noticed the maid whom I knew and whom the lady had mentioned to me. My heart began to throb (40) because I assumed that I was supposed to go to my lady who pleased me so much. But listen to what she did. The maid said the following: "Oh God, it is not going well for us (45), our happiness has left us. The master has returned to the house. My lady is so distraught about it that she can only cry. [606] But she told me, you should not be vexed about it: what cannot be now will happen another time."

I went with her up to the staircase, but good luck had abandoned me. At that moment I remembered something (5). I thought to myself: "Go back to the same spot [in the bedroom], squat down next to the wall where you had found the crack with your hand the other night and through which you had looked at her bed." (10) Indeed, I sat down at the same location and scanned the entire place, considering whether the situation was really the way the maid had described it to me.

Soon enough the young woman arrived (15), leading with her into the room the monk whom I had forbidden her to see. He lay down on the bed with her. There I sat, a very sad man. I reflected a short while (20) and then went to my friends. I said to them: "Now listen to this," and told them what had happened there. I also told them everything (25) I had experienced, from the very beginning to the end, and also what I had seen and heard the day before when I had looked through the wall, observing the old man on the bed (30). I also told them what she had promised me, and how, nevertheless, she had brought the monk in with her.

They took me by my hands and led me away from the wall.[5] Everyone mocked me (35). Good luck was not destined to fall upon me. They kept talking about me for a long time and finally pushed me so far that I lost my senses and sat on the ass [idiomatic expression = started to act like a fool] (40). I wanted to avenge everything that had happened to me by hitting and stabbing as is the custom among such people [who suffer such a fate]. We spent the whole night together. But I was still filled with great sorrow (45). By then mid-morning had arrived. My friends approached me and said: "We want to ride away because we do no longer want (50) to stay here. [607] It would be useless to leave you here behind. Do not object to this plan! After all, we are concerned that one day it might happen to you (5) that people would observe you in the same situation as the old man. You are not

[5] The narrator refers to the wall with the crack, but it is unclear how they had suddenly found themselves in that room.

clear in your mind: you are deceived by the woman. Please realize that, undoubt-edly (10), love has caught you with a fishing rod which the young woman holds [literally: which connects you with the young woman]. You do not understand with whom you are dealing, and you have also forgotten that yesterday you were sitting (15) behind the fireplace in the middle of the smoke, and how she treated you like a fool, and that she did not forgo the monk for you (20). Therefore do not say one word against our plan because we have never seen you, or ever will see you again, in this terrible shape that you are in right now (25). Therefore, come to your senses, you must leave with us!"

I sat there and thought about everything, whether I might achieve anything [with my lady] through anger or through begging (30). I looked for a good defense against my friends. They clearly noticed from my behavior that I was searching for such a strategy that would have allowed me to stay behind. This was my whole desire (35). Thereupon they said to me: "We are not going to let you do this. Get ready for dinner [idiomatic phrase = pack your stuff] so that we can get on the road together with you (40). This will be more useful for you than staying here and seeing every day what the woman and the monk are doing together, treating you like a fool." (45)

We discussed the matter at length, but I do not want to repeat everything. In short, they did not want to wait any longer, and I had to ride away with them.
[608]

If I were to tell you quickly what unhappiness filled me and what feelings I had in my heart, this would be nothing but a bothersome [literally: an entertain-ing] story for you, especially if I explained things in detail (5). Whether I were tell-ing this to strangers or friends, it would only bring shame upon myself. Therefore I prefer to let it go and allow each and everyone who has ever experienced in his life (10) that his heart was in flames and who felt love to judge this matter.

With this I want to stop and quickly come to the end, as everyone [obviously] desires (15).

We rode for a long time until we finally reached our home. As soon as we re-alized this, we all expressed the desire that no one should reveal this story (20), how it happened with us [especially with me]. We were welcomed by our families. This concludes this account.

Froben Christoph von Zimmern:[1]
"Der enttäuschte Liebhaber"

In ainer statt das geschach,
Die nit weit ligt von Ach,
Ains abents ich spacieren gieng,
An ainer gassen ich anfieng.

Ich gedacht: "Es ist noch frue,"   5
Stand ains still und lug zue,
Was schener jungkfrawen hie sind,
Mägt, weib und auch kindt,
Die alle nach wunsch sind geschaffen.

Ein menige von leien und von pfaffen   10
Standend auch an dem ring.
Da sich der tanz anfieng,
Sach ich ain raien oder zwen
Hin und her für mich gen,

Iedoch zuletst da nam ich war   15
Ains dürnlins, das was brun gefar;
Dasselb mir ganz mein herz besaß,
Ich wist weder diß noch das,
Was ich halten oder lassen sollt;

Das macht, das ich so schwitzlich holt   20
Allain demselben dürnlin was.

---

[1] The text was originally contained in the edition by Karl August Barack, ed., *Zimmerische Chronik*, vol. 1 (1881), 586–608. Hanns Fischer, ed., *Die deutsche Märendichtung des 15. Jahrhunderts*, 1961, also included this *mære*, and most recently, it can be found online at: http://de.wikisource.org/wiki/Zimmerische_Chronik#Projektfortschritt (last accessed on Sept. 19, 2006). Since this proves to be a most fascinating narrative, perhaps one of the true masterpieces of late-medieval German literature, but largely overlooked by scholarship, a complete edition of the original text seems appropriate here.

Ich gedächt: Ach Gott, der genaß,
Dem die frucht zu tails wurt;
Was im leidens darvon geburt,

Das sollt er alles achten klain.   25
Ich sach das türnlin steets allain.
Da ich sein also name war,
Ich erhub mich und macht mich dar.
Alsbald ich zu ime trat,

Nidersitzen es mich pat   30
Und grüeßt mich ser mit worten klug;
Wann das het endert fug,
So sach es mich gar lieplich an;
Ie mer und mer mein herze bran,

Das ich im zur selben stundt   35
Vor holtschaft kain wort nit reden kundt;
Doch plickt ich es hinwider an.
Das begund es bald an mir verstan;
Wiewol es was der jar ain kind,

So was es doch der sach nit blind,   40
Es sprach: "Gesell, hab mansmut!
Dein sach die möcht noch werden gut;
Ich sich, das du verirret bist
Von ainer lieb, die dir gebrist.

Ich pitt, sag mir dieselben that,   45
Villeucht so gib ich dir ain rath,
Der darzu wol erschießen mag.
Morn so wurts aber tag;
Was heut nit sy, das sy morn!

Dein truren das laß sein verlorn!   50
Ich sich dich fir getrewe an,
Darumb ich dir vil gutes gan."
Ich dank im zur selben stund,
Entschlossen gar het es min mund;

Mir was entschlagen do der ban.   55
Mein red die hub ich also an
Und sagt ir ganz den willen mein,
Wie sie mich hielt in großer pein;

Ob sie mir nit mit gnaden nig
Und mir ir trew und lieb verzig; 60
Mit lengern worten ich das thet,
Die sie von mir verstanden het.
Mit lachen sie mich ansach,

Gar spottlich zu mir do sprach:
"Gesell, hast du mich darfür, 65
Das ich gelich entschließ die thier
Gegen aim so frembden man,
Dess ich doch kund nie gewan?

Ich main, du seiest uß der affen land;
Sehe hin dir mein trew zu pfand, 70
Das du nit bist genug gelert
Der spur, die zu den dingen hört."
Sie sprach: "Du bist ain linder man,

Das du dich so bald magst nemen an
Fründtschaft zu aim frembden weib 75
Und sie darfst bitten umb irn leib;
Ich main, es habs der wein gethon,
Oder dein hürn das trübt der mon."

Zu ir sprach ich: "Fraw, zirnet nit!
Verniempt noch ainmal mein pitt! 80
Lasst euch nit so zornig sehen!
Es ist mir ganz in schimpf geschehen
Die wort, so ich geredt hab,

Und das erpüeten, so ich euch gab."
Ich wand, damit gebessert han, 85
Erst het ich groß unrecht gethan;
Ich wand, sie wellt mich han geschlagen.
Erst hub sie an ser ab mir clagen

Und sprach, ich wer ain bub von art,
Das ich nie wirs gehandelt ward. 90
Sie sprach: "Hastus gelesen in buchen,
Das man soll frawen also versuchen?
Pfui dich, der großen schant!

Man sollt dich nit lan im landt,
Das du so gar am rugken leist 95

Und ain er umb schand geist.
Du bist ain zerrichter man,
Es kompt dich von kaim guten an."

In dem kert sie sich von mir.
"Deins besitz ich wol embir."   100
Von angsten war mir haiß und kalt,
Die red die zwang mich mit gewalt,
Das ich nit wist, was ich thet,

Das ich die sach so gehandelt het.
Ich wist nit, was ich darzu sollt sagen.   105
"Der teufel hat mich daher tragen",
Sprach ich do wider mich.
Ob ich das nun widersprich

Und uf mein alte red kom,
Allererst möcht sie mich haißen nit from   110
Und sprechen, ich wer ains leichten mut;
Ich waiß nit, ob es taugen tut.

Do ich saß also gedenken,
Die sprach: "Schluraff, wie wilt henken
Din kopf so ganz uf die erden?   115
Bait noch ain weil! laß nacht werden!
Ich sich wol, das dich blanget

Nach wein, der dir für die augen hanget."
Sölcher spottwort sie mir vil gab.
Ich gedacht: "Nain, still dich heflich ab,   120
Dieweil es so gut ist gethan!
Du magst iezt nit bessers han."

Ich hub mich uf und gieng davon.
Man tanzt forthin, als ist gewon.
Ich stallt mich hindern tanz hindan;   125
Ganz trurig was ich gethan;
Ich het vil wechselsinn bei mir.

Iezo dacht ich, Gott wels füegen schier,
Das sie gedenk dich in gut.
Gleich so verkert sich mein mut.   130
"Ie, wie thust so derlich denken,
Das du ie nun ir stim willt lenken

Zu dem, das ir nit im herzen ist?
Wie bist so thor, das du vergist
Der wort, so sie het geredt? 135
Gang hinweg, leg dich zu bett!
Da stat dir vil mer gewins bei.

Du sichst wol ir wesen frei,
Sie hat lützel laid ab dir."
Allererst do begund mir 140
Mein har gen himel grislen
Und alles mein blut wislen,

Das ich kom verhub das wainen;
Ich must mich an ain wand lainen,
Das ich nit wol kund gestan. 145
"Was arbaitselliger, ellendiger man
Bin ich zu disen stunden,

Das mich ain weib hett so gebunden!"
Mit der sach ich also rang,
Die mich so genzlich bezwang; 150
Ich maint, mein leben müest erwinden,
Ob ich nit ir huld möcht vinden.

Do mein gedank was also ganz,
Von stund an zerließ sich der tanz;
Do wollt ich gar eben acht han, 155
Wo das tirnlin hin wollt gan.
Es zoch hin mit andern frawen.

Do begund ich wol ußchawen.
Als es kam für ain staine thor,
Daselbst pegegnet im vor 160
Ain junger münch in graw beklaidt.

Ich waiß nit, was er im seit.
Es nam seiner red gar eben war,
Damit warf es im s'mule dar,
Alda von in baiden ain schmutz. 165
Wie nach mir vor laid geschach zu kurz,

Dess mag ain iedes hermessen,
Dem liebe sein herz hat besessen.
Ich stund als ain unwissender still;

Ich main, es ergieng ir will,   170
Wan ich was so btoren,

Das ich sie hett verloren;
Ich wust nit, wa sie kommen war;
Mir ward in vil jar
Der weil nit so langen.   175
Erst kament sie gegangen,

Ich waiß litzel, waher,
Ob sie kemen uß dem ker,
Oder wa sie wern gesessen,
Dess bin ich ganz vergessen.   180
[1439] In dem kam ain alter man

Uß dem hus fürher gan,
Der hett wol gesehen,
Das der schmutz was geschehen.
Wa er darnach hin wer kommen,   185
Oder was er mer hat vernommen,

Das kan mir nit wissendt sein,
Dann mich irret der sonnen pein.
Do er das dirnlin anesach,
Mögt ir heren, was er sprach: 190
"Mätzlin, wa seit ir gewesen?

Habt ir aber alles ufgelesen,
So krumb es uf der gassen lit?
Ob ich hie erhubt den stritt,
Das brächt mir klainen frommen.   195
Ich verzeih, biß wir haim kommen."

Do ich die red also vernam,
Ich waiß nit, wa der münch hinkam.
Das metzlin hub sich hinfür,
Ich folgt im biß zu der thür,   200
Do gieng es hinein.

Daran stund die herberg mein,
Darin ich zu huse was;
Do ward mir vil dess baß,
Do ich im so nahent huset,   205
Wiewol mir doch gruset,

Als ir vor wol hand gehert,
Wie die gespillschaft ward zerstert.
Ains löffens ich do luf
Schneblenclich die stegen uf   210

Und gedacht, ob ich mit fugen
Ienderthin überlugen
Oder heren, was da wellt werden.
Ich such embor und uf der erden,
Ob ich iendert ain lechlin fund.   215

Zu letst do ward mir kund
Ain spalt an ainer wand;
Den begraif ich mit meiner hand.
Ich satzt mich dran und wollt schawen,
Ob ich iendert seh die frawen,   220

Die mir vor so wol gefallen hett.
Als ich so umb mich lugen tät,
So ersich ich die liebsten mein:
Gar nach verschwunden was min pein;
Dann das mir alles inne lag,   225

Das ich gesehen het bei tag,
Do mir der münch in garten trat.
Wie mit klainem fleiß ich in das pat!
Ich gab im auch dess klainen sold,
Das er der were hold,   230

Die ich von herzen lieben thet.
Wenig ir ich das trawet het
Nach den worten, die sie mir gab.
Zu diesem zeil steck ich mein stab
Und mach mich wider uf die straßen,   235

Da ich die red vor hab gelassen.
An die wand schmuckt ich mich dar
Und wolt vil bas nemen war,
Was sich da wellt heben an
Vom dirnlein und vom alten man.   240

Nun was es kommen uf das zil,
Das der vinsteri kam so vil
Von der nacht, das geschach,

Das ich nit wol hindurch sach.
Do waiß ich nit, was im gezam,   245

Gar bald es mit aim liechtlin kam;
Das stackt es neben sich embor,
Darzu ain schatt, der stund darvor.
Das dirlin gieng zu dem bett;
Wie bald es sich usschlaufen thet,   250

Es legt sich an das bett hinan.
In dem so kumpt der alte man
Gegangen zu der kammer in,
Schummet als ain eberschwin;
Kriegens in nit verdroß.   255

Mit dem er die thür beschloß.
In klaidern legt er sich uf das bet,
Als ob er ain grose krankheit het.
Da er das dirnlin anesach,

Mögt ir hören, was er sprach: 260
"Du waist wol, metzlin, was hast gethon;
Was soll ich dir darumb geben zu lon?
Ich hab dir den münch dick gewert
Und auch dein leib darumb erbert;

Das hilft recht, als es mag.   265
Morn so wurts der fierte tag,
Das ich dich darumb straffen thet.
Ich legt auch vleisig an dich mein pät
Und versucht es mit güte an dich;

Das hat als geholfen nichts;   270
Du magst der alten tik nit lon,
Den münchen bist du underthon."
Das dürnlin sich umbkeren thet,
Als ob es fast geschlaffen het,

Und sprach zum alten man: 275
"Du hast mich gelogen an;
Wiltu die rechten warhait jehen,
So hast mich uf dem münch gesehen
Und nit den münch uf mir;

Das sag ich in rechter warhait dir." 280
Mit dem kert es sich wider umb,
Schwigendt, als ob es wer ain stumb.
Allererst sach ich ain grusen man,
Das im sein herz vor zoren bran.

Mengen fluch er dem tirnlin thet, 285
Das sich darab nit verharmdet hett;
Wie laut er ob im schwur und rief,
Nit minder täts, als ob es schlief.
Der red der traib er also vil,

Die ich euch nit halber nemmen will, 290
Dann es wurd sich lengen.
In dem so begund sich mengen
Der zorn und die liebin,
Die er hett zum dirnlin.

Da er wand, es wer entschlaffen, 295
Da hub er an sein har ußraufen
Und sprach: "Ach ewiger Gott,
Wie ist es mir ain schand und spott,
Das ich die schmach ansehen soll!

So mag es auch nit haben wol 300
An dem futter, das ich im gib;
Und söllt es machen mit dem sib,
So wer es mer dann halber staub.
Ei, wie bin ich so taub!

Seit es nit anheut erwint, 305
Ain vih gat, da es zu essen findt.
Ich kan im darumb nit find sin,
Wann es hat ganz das herze min.

Ee ich von ime wellte lan,
Ich wellt im ehe ußer wege gan." 310
Der red von ime ward vil verbracht.
Es nahet sich gen mittenacht,
Das im zu schlaffen auch gezam.

Sin zorn der was im worden lam.
Das dirnlin das bedacht sich bas, 315
Da er allererst entschlaffen was:

Es kert sich gegen im gar schnell,
Ain schrai ließ es, der was hell;

Es sprach: "Du mein liebster hort,
Du hast gethan an mir ain mort,   320
Das du des nachts nit nider gest,
Iez du mich ser erschrecket hest."
Userm schlaff der alt erschrack,

"Pfei dich, du verfliechter sack!
Warum schraustu nit also,   325
Do der münch dich hett im stro
Und mit dir sin willen hett
Dort an ainer vinstren stett?

Du must noch darumb verderben
Und villeucht darzu ersterben!"   330
Das dirnlin zu dem alten sprach,
Da es in also ligen sach:
"Ei, du mein liebster man,

Du hast mir warlich unrecht than:
Von mir hastus nit gesehen,   335
Es ist dir im trom geschehen,
Ich het nie kain man zu dir,
Das soltu frei glauben mir;

Und wist ich, das dus in ernst thetest,
Auch das vertrawen zu mir hettest,   340
Ich wollt auch nit biß morgen beiten,
Nit mer kem ich an dein seiten."
Damit thet es sich ufs kise lainen,

Mit haisen zeher begund es wainen,
Darzu ser seine hende winden.   345
"Kain mentsch soll mich nit also finden,
Ob Gott will!" sprach das dirnlin
Zu dem alten manne sein.

Do hub an der alt und sprach:
"Kain felscher weib ich nie gesach,   350
Die will mich mit worten schenden
Und mit offnen augen blenden.
Du waist, als ich necht kummen bin,

Das ganz erzürnt was mein sinn,
Und das ich dich darumb straffen thet   355
Der that ich ie gesehen hett,
Und wilt mich iez mit worten laichen;
Ich sage dir zu wortzaichen:
Wie der münch dir gab den segen

Und wie er wer uf dir gelegen,   360
Da antwurtest du zur stund
Und kumbst mit aim sollichen fundt
(Ich bin der sach noch nit vergessen),
Du werest uf dem münch gesessen,

Und der münch nit uf dir.   365
Noch mer sagtest mir,
Du wondest bei dem Barfuoßer ligen,
So war ain Prediger zu dir gedigen;
Die red die thetstu mit mir treiben,

Darum so laß es am nechsten bleiben!"   370
Allererst do hub sich jamer und mort.
Das dirnlin wandt sich uf ain ort
Und hub an wainen und clagen
Mit worten, als ich euch will sagen:

we, o we, mir vil armen,   375
Das es Gott wol erbarmen
Solch unrecht, das mir geschicht
Von ainem solchen falschen wicht!
Wenn er sich überlet mit wein,

So verliert er die stime sein,   380
Als dir iezo ist geschehen.
Nechten bistu wenig gesehen,
Das du kum hast künnen gen,
Darzu nit am ainli stän;

Das ist an dem wol schein,   385
Du ligst noch als ain schwein;
Dess magst du nit mit warhait fliehen,
Dann du kunt dich necht nit abziehen.
Wann ich dich wolt niderfüeren,

So begegnest du mir mit schwüren   390
Und mit solchem schelten,

Dess ich arme fraw muß entgelten.
Wann dir alsdann ain trom erscheint,
Als dir ist geschehen heint,

Da dein sinn ist mit wein besessen,   395
Dann wilts als zum ergsten messen
Und tust nit dann schreien und ruofen
Gleich aim unstimmigen wuofen.
Die warheit ist mir nit verzigen,

Du thust noch also da ligen   400
Und schmeckst als ain essigvaß;
Mir werd wirs oder bas.
Hilft mir Gott, das es wurt tag
Und das ich gen mag!

Ich wolt mich selbs ehe erdrenken   405
Oder an ain stang erhenken,
Ehe ich das leiden well;
Mir wer baß in der hell,

Dann also hederisch leben.
Dess will ich dir mein trew geben."   410
Uf das sie ain zittern gewan,
Als ob sie fieber wer kommen an,
Und verkert damit die augen;

Ich sag es one laugen,
Sie thet, als ob sie tod wer.   415
Lachens ich ganz verber;
Ob ich noch also ains sollt schawen
Ainen man, ich geschwig ainer frawen

So will ich sein lieber emberen
Und anderer kurzweil geren.   420
In dem der alt seer erschrack,
Da das dirnlin also lag.
Das kam von zwaien schulden,

Von vorcht und von hulden;
Er wond, es wer also,   425
Als sie gebarete do,
Das er schuld an irem sichtum hett
Und das er sie müeße heben zu bett;

Auch was er im so herzlich hold,
Das er dhains fürsten sold,   430
Den er für sie het genommen,
Das er umb sie sollt sein kommen.
Do sie ain wenig zu ir selbs kam,

Ir hand in die seinen er do nam
Und sprach also zu ir: 435
"Wolltest du glauben mir,
So sprüch ichs wol uf meinen aid,
Es ist mir sicherlichen laid

Alles das, so dir gebrist,
Der krankhail, das du inne bist."   440
Das dirnlin do gar senfte sprach,
Do es den alten anesach :
"Hab ich noch nit gnug bin,

Das du erst wilt spotten min
Zu dem leiden und schmerzen,   445
Den ich trag an meinem herzen,
Damit du mich iez tust pfenden?
Dann mein leben will sich enden."

In dem sank es aber dahin,
Als ob es sein letztes wellte sin.   450
Do der gris diß sach also,

Wie lut er schrai: "Mordio,
Soll ich nun verlieren die?
Ich mag nit mer leben hie,
Dann ich wird gar zu nicht   455

Ab ir end, das geschicht."
Das und vil anders mee
Redt der alt user grosem wee.
"Ach herr Gott, laß geschehen,

Das ich sie gesund mög sehen!   460
Ich will dir bei meinem leben
Alle jar ain zins geben.
Auch hilf mir, lieber herre
Sant Jacob, der verre!

Ich gib dir auch ain gabe,   465
Hilf mir der sorg abe!"
Alsbald er dess verhaisen het,
Das dirnlin ain aug ufthet,
Als ob es wer erkecket

Und von dem tod erwecket.   470
Do der alt ersahe das,
An seinem herzen ward im bas,
Sein hand hub er uf gen Gott:
"Ach milter herr, durch dein gebott

Bistu, wer getrawet dir;   475
Du hast auch geholfen mir,
Das ich dir immer dank sag,
Als lang ich geleben mag!"
Er thet sich do zum dirnlin.

"Ach herzallerliebste min,   480
Ich mag es für ain warhait jehen,
Es ist ain groß zaichen geschehen
Hit zu tag an dir,
Darvon billichen wir

Gott sollent eren   485
Und sein lobe meren."
Nu megt ir heren, was geschach.
Das dirnlin zu dem alten sprach:
"Ich sollt sein gestorben,

So het mir erworben   490
Sant Jacob das leben mein.
Noch so leidt ich pein,
Die du mir hest zugefiegt;
Damit dich noch nit benüegt:

Du treipst mit mir deinen spott.   495
Es bleib nit ongestraft von Gott,
Es werd dir darumb der lon,
Dann du hast mir unrecht thon
Dess, so du mich hast gezigen."

In dem do begund nigen   500
Der alt zu dem dirnlein:

"Ich pitt, verstand die red mein!
Du sollt warlich wissen,
Ich will sein geflissen,

Dich in er und gut setzen   505
Und dich deins laids ergetzen;
Dann ich kan wol verston,
Das ich dir unrecht hett thon;

Es soll dir fürhin nit me schaden,
Ob ich mit win wurd so bladen.   510
Das ich aber ain sollichs wenen wellt,
So sy es zu meiner torhait zellt!
Darum so setz ichs ganz zu dir;

Biß füro ungestraft von mir!"
Und schankt im ain klainat do,   515
Des ward das dirnlin harde fro.
"Noch will ich dir ains geben:
Du magst nach deinem willen leben
Und selbs immer maister sein,
Das hab dir für die pein   520
Und auch für das zu lon,
Das ich dir unrecht hab gethon!"
Do sprach das dirnlin gar schlecht:

"Das du mir dick so unrecht
Deinen zorn hast gegeben,   525
Es kurzt mir mein leben,
Das ich dester ehe sterben muß.
Noch so gehert uf buß,

Das man soll vergeben die tat,
Die dann ains gesundet hat;   530
Darum dweil du die schuld nennest
Und dich des unrechten bekennest,
So thur dich hernigen,

Ich will dir verzigen
Und mit dir haben son,   535
Das dus nit mer wellest thon."
Darauf sprach der alte gris:
"Herzlieb, ich pitt dich mit fliß,

Das du dess nit mer wellest gedenken,
So will ich dir ganz anhenken   540
Die schlüssel zu dem, so ich han,
Das soll dir sein alles underthan."
Uf das nam es in in seine arm.

Das macht dem alten kalt und warm,
Es macht auch uß aim man ain kindt,   545
Darzu mit offnen augen blindt;
Dann er gedächt, der will wer gut.
Das sterkt dem alten seinen mut,

Und hett damit ganz vergessen,
Was im vor sein herz het bsessen,   550
Auch des schmachs, den er hett vernommen,

Was im ganz uß sinnen kommen.
Damit so ward die sach geschlicht
Und aller handel genzlich gericht.
Der alt sich zu dem dirnlin legt,   555
Sein kommer der ward ganz wett
Von der liebe manigfalt,

Die doch was im dirnlin kalt;
Wiewol es da den gleichen thet,
Als ob es ganz zu dank het.   560
Noch was er im zu aller stund
Ain surer apfel in den mundt;

Dess ließ es doch nit merken sich.
Ie zuweil gab es ain stich
Dem alten mit den augen;   565
Es kondt gar tougen
Mit dem alten umbgen

Und im farben stim wen.
Do es in ganz gefasst hett,
Mögt ir heren, was er thet.   570
Es hub sein wort also an:
"Herzallerliebster man,

Ich wöllt dir gern entschließen,
Wo es dich nit wellt verdrießen,
Das es gar umbsunst ist gethan,   575

Wo ains weibs furcht der man;
Dann es ist ain alt gesprochen wort,

Das du dick hast gehort:
Es ist die aller best hut
Die, so ain fraw selbst thut;   580
Dann wa aine nit selbs hüeten will,
Da hilft weder litzel noch vil.

Noch muß ich dir me ains sagen,
Was geschach vor langen tagen:
In der edlen statt Prato   585
Was ain gesetz also,
Das ain iedtlichs weib

Hett verloren iren leib,
Dess half sie nichts uf erden,
Sie musst verbrennt werden;   590
Es dienet auch nit weiter me;
Dann, welche brach ir ehe,

Auch besunder, wo das geschach,
Das man miet oder glaub anfacht.
Nun in derselben statt   595
Gar kurz sich begeben hat,
Das ain edle junge fraw alda,

Genannt die schen Philippa,
Von irem mann, Rinaldo genannt,
In irer kammer ain jungling fand.   600
Der was auch von edlem stammen
Und hieß Lazarino mit nammen,
Schlief bei der schenen frawen am bett,

Den sie als sich selbs lieb hett,
Mit armen und bain umbfangen;   605
Ich main, es wer hergangen
Ir baider will zur stunden.
Das sie ir man also hat funden,

Darvon großen kommer nam,
Das er nach von sinnen kam   610
Und an aim klainen erwinden tät,
Das er sie nit baid ertötet hett;
Doch auch ainsthails darum borget,

Das er sich vor dem jungen besorget,
Und damit pariret,   615
Sein zorn auch temperiret,
Doch sich nit ganz meßigen kundt.
Er bedacht an derselben stundt
Der vorgenannten statut und recht.
Er berueft seine mägt und auch knecht   620
Und sust ander leut vil,
Das sie kemen uf das zil.
Die ließ er alle da anschawen,

Wie lag der jungling bei der frawen,
Umb das obs not thet.   625
Das er sie zu zügen hett.
Nun alsbald sich der tag ufbürt,
Der man sein weib für gericht fürt.

Als nun die fraw fürs gericht kam,
Gar bald sie in im sinn nam   630
Ain starken, vesten mut,
Es sy bes oder gut.
So fasst sie dann zu kurzer frist,

Als nach der bulerin gewonhait ist.
Uf das sie gar freulich ufblicket.   635
Bald nach iren lieben fründen sie schücket,
Die bat sie umb ret,
Wie sie sich fristen thet,

Das sie nit wurd geschendt
Und darzu mit feur verbrent.   640
Die ir rieten mit solchen klenken,
Sie sollt sich uß gehe bedenken,
Damit von dem gericht weichen

Und gar verr hinweg schleichen.
Das war ir sonder gefallen,   645
Dien rat fand sie on inen allen.
Ein gute weil sie also uf ir selb stund,
Sie tät, als noch starke gemüeth thund.

Darauf sich gar kurz beriet,
Von ir aller red sie schied   650
Und wellt ie für recht kommen,
Es brächt ir schaden oder frommen,

Und mit starkem gemüt sterben,
Dann mit ligender frucht verderben

Und ehe sie in verlaugnen thet,   655
In dess ann sie geschlaffen het.
Do sie sich so bedacht hat,
Gar schnell sie für den richter trat.
Als sie nun für den richter kam,

Ain frei, freulich gemüet sie an sich nam,   660
Den richter do fragen begon,
Was sie schuldiget der man.
Der richter ain frommer, redlicher man was,
Hub uf und sagt ir das,

Wie ir man sein clag thun het   665
Und wie er den jungling an dem bett
In iren armen het funden schlaffen,
Darumb so müeßt er straffen
Nach der statt statut und recht,

'Soverr ir das nit widersprecht;   670
Dann ewer man schuldigt euch der tat;
Darvor so lugt, was ir zu schaffen hat!"
Die fraw unerschrockenlich den richter ansach,
Züchtig, demüetig und lieplich sprach:

'Herr, der richter, ich leugen dess nit,   675
Ich lag hint Lazerino mit
Ganzer fründtlicher liebe bei,
Das es mich gerowen sei,
Dess einst es warlichen nit gethan,

Dann ich waiß in der welt kain man,   680
Dem ich größer liebe trag;
Die mert sich von tag zu tag.
Aber noch verniempt ain wort mein:
Herr richter, euch solt wol wissendt sein,

Das alle gestetzt, statut und recht   685
Sollent sein also schlecht;
Sie seien groß oder klain,
So sond sie doch sein gemain.
Sie sond sich auch geleichen

Dem armen als dem reichen,   690
Der frawen als dem man,
Solches billich eben stan;
Das wer ain statut gut,
Die alda nit erscheinen thut,

Dann allain die frawen und nit man   695
Dem gesatz sollent sein underthan.
Das bedunkt mich sein ain spott
Und auch darzu wider Gott;
Dann ir man hend diß satzung gemacht

Und habend dabei nie gedacht,   700
Kain frawen darzu zu nemen.
Wie wol mag sich das gezimen,
Das wir weiber hie uf erden

Und nit ir man gebüst werden?
Darumb so sprüch ich wol frei,   705
Das ewer statut nit recht sei.
Do wie und was man well,
Wend ir euer seel in die hell

Umb meinen leib geben
Und mir nemen das leben,   710
Das steet wol zu ewerm gwalt.
Noch hat die sach ain gestalt,
Wellt euch das gezemmen,

Das ir die wellt vernemen
Und euch so lang entwellen,   715
Biß ich die möcht erzellen,
Das ist, das ir fragt mein man,
Ob ich im nie gefellt hab daran,
Das ich im nit gehorsam sy gesein;
Wann er hab begert mein,   720
So was ich allweg geschickt;

Wie oft und wie dick
Er das an mich muten thet,
So hab ich ims nie verseit.'
Uf das der man anhub und sprach: 725
'Herr richter, sie hat war an der sach,
Ich hab sollichs nie an sie begert,
Sie hab mich dess von stund gewert.'

Alsbald der man die red verbracht,
Gar kurz sich die fraw bedacht   730
Und sprach zu dem richter do:
'Hett nun mein man also
Sin notturft zu aller zeit gehapt von mir,

Genzlich nach allen sins herzen gir,
War soll ich dann das thon,   735
Das er nit nutzen kan?
Soll ich es dann zu stund
Hinwerfen für die hund?

Ist es dann nit besser gethan,
Ich geb es ainem jungen edelman   740
Und werd im zu willen mit,
Dweil er mich darum pitt,
Und besonder eim, da es also stat,

Der mich me, dann sich lieb hat?
Dunkt mich ie bas sein geton,   745
Dann sollichs verderben lon.'
Nun warend vil von mannen und frawen,
Die alle begunden anzuschawen

Und sich an den ring gestellt,
Besehen, was da werden well.   750
Als nun die fraw da an der steet
Ir kurzweilig, abenteurig red getet
Und ir antwurt also erschein,
Do ward von allem volk gemain
Zu dem richter also geredt,   755
Das die fraw zumal recht het,
Und mit kurzen worten schlecht

So hett ir man ganz unrecht;
Und schreien auch zum richter,
Die gesetz weren zu schwer;   760
Darvor so sollt im gezimmen
Und das recht abnemen;

Das sollt also werden gesetzt,
Damit die weib wurden geletzt,
Das man die straffen söllt,   765
Die das theten umbs gelt.
Do diß alles so geschach

Und der man anesach,
Das er schand und spott empfieng,
Bald von dem rechten weg gieng.   770
Die sehen fraw freelichen stund,
Als noch zu tag leut thund,

Die hie uf erden
Vom todt erlest werden.
Gar zichtigclich sie die straf fieng   775
Und damit wider zu haus gieng."
Das dirnlin do uf im selber saß.

Es besint sich ain wenig baß,
Gar seiner da hub es wider an
Und sprach als zu dem alten man: 780
"Herzlieb, ains das frag ich dich,
Hastu nun verstanden mich

Dess, so ich dir hab erzelt,
So sag mir, wies dir gefellt."
Der alt sich zu dem metzlin naig,   785

Als ob er schlief, und schwaig.
Über lang erst da hub er an,

Als er sich gar wol besan,
Und sprach do zum dirnlin:
"Ich laß es alles eben sin,   790
Dann was ich dir zugesagt hab,
Da will ich dir nit prechen ab."

Das bedunkt das metzlin recht,
Damit ward der herr zum knecht
Also nach alten esseln geschehen soll,   795
Das ist gar billich und wol,
Die kum mögen gen gemach

Und doch wellen laufen umb scharlach.
Das laß ich stan zu diser frist
Und eben sein, wie das ist,   800
Nit me will ich davon sagen.
In dem do begund es tagen,
Da wir wurden ufsten.

Mit dem musst ich dannen gehn,
Damit man nit merken thet,   805
Was ich alda vernommen hett.
Nim wellen heren, was ich sag!
Es bestund biß nach mittem tag,

Ich saß als vor dem haus,
Ob es indert wellt gen herauß,   810
Das ich mein red gen im thet
Und es aber fründtlich pet,
Damit im erzaigt mein not,

Als uf dem alten schrot,
Gleich als Engeleiers knecht,   815
Wiewol meine wort warendt schlecht.
Doch ich also ainig saß
Und mich alda besinnet baß,

So blück ich gen seiner thür.
In dem kam es gangen herfür   820
Und sprach zu mir, wess ich da säß.
"Ach fraw, und wer es euch gemeß,
Und wellt gar kurz tagen

Und euch mein mainung sagen:
Ich sitz durch ewern willen do,   825
Ir mögt mich laidig und fro
Machen, ob ir gebieten mir;
In ewerm dienst so wurd ich schier

Erlöst gar von aller pein;
Nun merkt ir wol den willen mein."   830
Sie sprach zu mir: "Du kompst mir recht,
Ich hab mangel an ainem knecht.
Der hacken und reiten kund

In miner wissen, wann ich ims gund;
Darzu müeßtest ußchawen,   835
Das du kendest holz hawen
Und ander ruhe arbait vil,
Die ich dir iezt nit nemmen will,"

Und hub damit an zu lachen.
Ich verstund mich nit der sachen,   840

Ob ir wer ernst oder schimpf.
Sie kond auch nit mit glimpf
Lenger bei mir sten;

Sie ward fürußgehn.
Ich saß wie vor gedenken: 845
"Wie mit abenteurlichen schwenken

Ist das weib beladen gar!
Ich main, ain ganze gauggelerschar
Ir nit gelichen kunde.
Das sie mir ir lieb gunde!   850
So wer mir geschehen wol;
Sehnen nach ir macht mich dol
Und benimpt mir all mein macht,
Das ich weder tag noch nacht
Kain ruhe nit mag gehan."   855
In dem kam sie wider her gan
Und sprach: "Du gesell" zu mir,

"Ains will ich sagen dir:
Ich hab vor wol verstanden dich,
Wie du gern bsprechest mich;   860
Nun ist mir auch also;
Ich sag dir, wie und wo

Du must suchen ain sölchen list:
In dem hus, da du zu herberg bist,
Hinder dem kemmin   865
Da sollt du warten min;
So gen ich in mein haus zu hand

Zu dir an dieselben wand;
Da ist ain alt, finster loch,
Sichst mich nit, so hörst mich doch."   870
In dem gieng sie bald für
Hinein zu ir thür.
Ich hub mich auch bald zu hand,
Da ich, das kemin vand,
Und setzt mich da nider.   875
Ich hab weder vor noch sider
Nie wirs zeit gehet,

Dann mir der rauch thet;
Und hett ich Nerons sündt gethan,

Ich möcht sie da gebüßet han.   880
Biß zu nacht saß ich da.
Wie dick dacht ich: "Wa

Ist das loch oder wann kompt sie har?
Ich main, das sie mit gefar
Mich daher gesetzet hab.   885

Ach Gott, nem es noch ab,
Das sie zu mir keme gan!"

Ich wellts als für ain schimpf han.
In dem kam sie zu mir,
"Ach Gott, wie gät es dir?   890
Es hat mir so wehe gethan,
Das ich dich allain han gelan;

Ich was so ganz bladen,
Das ich nit ainen vaden
Nit hett mögen spinnen;   895
Mein man der was hinnen.
Der ist iezo gegangen uß

Und kompt hint nit ins hus;
Darumb so will ich dich laden
Zu mir in mein gaden;   900
Dahin will ich dich setzen
Und dich laids ergetzen;
Dann ich sag dir uf diser fart,

Das mir kain mentsch nie lieber ward."
Ich sprach: "Das will ich wol sehen,   905
Ob ain ding will geschehen,
Das ist, das du nit me
Mit dem münch schaffest, als ehe,

Noch mit im redest ain wort."
Sie sprach: "Du mein höchster hort,   910
Ich will dir mein trew geben,
Das ich bei allen mim leben
Nimer mit im reden will,

Weder lützel noch vil,
Dess soltu von mir sicher sein   915
Uf die ganzen trewe mein!

Darumb so magst ain weilest gon,
So will ich dich wol wissen lon

Und dir schicken main maid,
Die dir die rechten warhait sait.   920
Damit so wellest hingan
Und uf die maid acht han!"
Mit dem bott sie mir die hand

Durch das loch in der wand.
Ich macht mich in jen kemmet,   925
Allda der würt bedecket het
Den tist, als man essen wollt.
Ich setzt mich do, als ich sollt,

Zu meinen gesellen an den tisch;
Es wer hüener oder visch,   930
Gar nichts ich dess achten tet;
Das schuf die freud, die ich do hett.
Gar bald verkert sich da mein mut.

Man hub uf, als man denn thut,
Das wasser ward getragen dar,   935
Von der tür da nam ich war
Der magt, die mir was bekannt,
Als sie die fraw mir hett genannt.

Mein herz das wischt mir uf im leib,
Ich wond, ich sollt gen zu dem weib,   940
Die mir so wol gefallen thät.
Nun mögt ir heren, was sie thet.
Die maidt die hub mit worten an:

"Ach Gott, es will uns übel gan,
Unser freud die ist hint uß,   945
Der herr ist kommen in das hus,
Und ist mein fraw so übel dran,
Das sie nichts dann weinen kan;

Doch spricht, ir sollts nit haben qual,
Was ietzt nit, sy ain andermal."   950
Ich gieng mit ir biß an die stegen;
Glicks des hett ich mich verwegen.
In dem do fiel mir eins in sinn,
Ich gedacht: "Nun macht dich wider hin

Und setz dich an die wand, 955
Do du den spalt mit der hand
Funden hast vornächt,

Da du uf ir bettlin sächt."
Alda setzt ich mich nider
Und sach hin und wider, 960
Ob das alles wer also,
Wie mir die magt sagt aldo.

Gar bald do kam das dirnlin
Und fürt den münch mit im hinein,
Den ich im vor verbotten hett. 965
Der legt sich zu im an das bett.
Da saß ich als ain trurig man.

Ain klaine weil ich mich besan
Und gieng nach meinen gesellen dar,
Ich sprach zu in: "Nun nement war!" 970
[1448] Und zaiget inen do die tat,
Die sich alda begeben hat.
Ich sagt inen auch die mer,
Wie es mir ergangen wer
Von anfang gar biß an das end, 975
Und was ich vor an der wend
Gesehen und gehert het

Mit dem alten an dem bett;
Auch was es mir hett zugesait
Und den münch darüber zu im glait. 980
Do namen sie mich bei der hand
Und fürten mich hin von der wand;

Sie wurdend alle spotten mein,
Es sollt mir nit geschehen sein.
Der wort der tribents also vil 985

Und brächten mich zu dem zil,
Das ich meiner sinn vergaß

Und ganz uf dem esel saß.
Die ding die wollt ich alle rechen,
Baide mit hawen und mit stechen, 990
Als noch ist solcher lüten sitt.
Die nacht vertriben wir damit.

Noch saß ich in grosen sorgen,
Es nacht sich gen mitlem morgen,
Do kamend meine gesellen   995
Und sprechend: "Wir wellen
Hinweg reiten
Dann wir nit beiten
Lenger hier mögen;

Es wurd auch nit tögen,   1000
Ob wir dich hie ließen.
Das laß dich nit verdriesen!
Dann wir haben dess sorgen,

Es begegnet dir morgen,
Das du auch wurdest gesehen,   1005
Als dem alten ist geschehen;
Dann dir iezo gebrist,
Das du betöret bist;

Dann die lieb on mangel
Dich gefasst hat an angel,   1010
Die du zu dem dirnlin hast,
Das du nit weist, wamitu umb gast,
Und werest auch dess vergessen,

Wie du hint bist gesessen
Hinderm kemin am rauch,   1015
Und wie es dich für ain gauch
Umb triben hat,
Und das es nit lat

Den münch durch dich.
Darumb nit sprich   1020
Ain wort darwider;
Dann vor noch sider
Haben wir dich so gesehen,

Als dir iezo ist geschehen.
Darum so nim dir dann sin,   1025
Du must mit uns hin!"
Ich saß also gedenken,
Ob ich iendert möcht lenken

Mit zorn oder mit gebet,
Das ich mich abreden thet.   1030
Sie sahend wol an meiner geberd,
Das ich sucht ain solliche geverd,
Da nur ich da bliben wer:

Das was genzlichen mein gär.
Do sprachend sie zu mir: 1035
"Wir folgend als nit dir,
Mach dich uf zum essen,
Das wir uf die straßen

Mit ainandern kommen!
Das bringt dir me frommen,   1040
Dann das du legest hie
Und teglich sehest, wie
Das dürnlin und der münch teten

Und dich für ain narren hetten."
Der red triben wir also vil,   1045
Die ich hie nit erzellen will;
Kurz, sie wollten nit mer baiten,
Ich musst mit inen reiten.

Ob ich nur vast erzellen thet,
Wie unmut mich besessen hett   1050
Und wie mir am herzen wer,
Das doch dir ain schimpflich mär,
Ob ich das tet ußkünden;

Es wer gegen frembden oder fründen,
So wer es mir selbs schmach gethon.   1055
Darumb so will ichs bleiben lon
Und aim ieden zu messen geben,
Dem ihe bei allen seim leben

Ist sein herz embrannt
Und der liebe worden bekannt.   1060
Dabei ichs iezo lassen will
Und il hin zu dem zil,
Damit iemandts blang.

Wir ritten so lang,
Biß wir haim kommen.   1065

Alsbald wir das vernommen,
Was unser aller beger,
Das kainer sagte die mer,

Wie es uns wer ergangen.
Also wurden wir empfangen,   1070
Ieder von seinem hausgenoß,
Damit sich die sach beschloß.

Bibliography

SOURCES

Cramer. *Maeren-Dichtung*, ed. Thomas Cramer. Spätmittelalterliche Texte 1–2. Munich: Fink, 1972.

Enikel. *Jansen Enikels Werke*, ed. Philipp Strauch. Monumenta Germaniae Historica, Scriptores Qui Vernacula Lingua Usi Sunt 3. Deutsche Chroniken und andere Geschichtsbücher des Mittelalters 3. Hanover and Leipzig: Hahnsche Buchhandlung, 1900.

Fischer. *Schwankerzählungen des deutschen Mittelalters*, sel. and trans. Hanns Fischer. Munich: Hanser, 1967.

———. *Die deutsche Märendichtung*. Münchener Texte und Untersuchungen zur deutschen Literatur des Mittelalters 12. Munich: Beck, 1966.

Grubmüller. *Novellistik des Mittelalters: Märendichtung*, ed., trans. and comm. by Klaus Grubmüller. Bibliothek des Mittelalters 23. Frankfurt a. M.: Deutscher Klassiker Verlag, 1996.

Hagen. *Gesammtabenteuer: Hundert altdeutsche Erzählungen: Ritter- und Pfaffen-Mären, Stadt- und Dorfgeschichten, Schwänke, Wundersagen und Legenden*, meist zum erstenmal gedruckt und herausgegeben von Friedrich Heinrich von der Hagen. 3 vols. 1850; Darmstadt: Wissenschaftliche Buchgesellschaft, 1961.

Kully and Rupp. *Der münch mit dem genßlein: 13 spätmittelalterliche Verserzählungen*. Aus dem Codex Karlsruhe 408 herausgegeben und erläutert von Rolf Max Kully und Heinz Rupp. Stuttgart: Reclam, 1972.

Schmid, Ursula. *Codex Vindobonensis 2885*. Bibliotheca Germanica 26. Deutsche Sammelhandschriften des späten Mittelalters. Bern and Munich: Francke, 1985.

Meyer, Otto Richard. *Der Borte des Dietrich von der Glezze: Untersuchungen und Text*. Heidelberg: Winter, 1915.

———. *Codex Karlsruhe 408*. Bibliotheca Germanica: Handbücher, Texte und Monographien aus dem Gebiete der germanischen Philologie 16; Deutsche Sammelhandschriften des späten Mittelalters. Bern: Francke, 1974.

Spiewok. *Altdeutsches Decamerone*, ed. and trans. Wolfgang Spiewok. 2nd ed. Berlin: Ruetten & Loening, 1984.

Zimmerische Chronik, ed. Karl August Barack. 2nd improved ed. 4 vols. Freiburg i. Br. and Tübingen: J. C. B. Mohr, 1881.

Die Chronik der Grafen von Zimmern: Handschriften 580 und 581 der Fürstlich Fürstenbergischen Hofbibliothek Donaueschingen, ed. Hansmartin Decker-Hauff and (since vol. 2) Rudolf Seigel. 3 vols. Constance and Stuttgart: Jan Thorbecke, 1964–1972.

CRITICAL STUDIES

Bastress-Dukehart, Erica. *The Zimmern Chronicle: Nobility, Memory and Self-Representation in Sixteenth-Century Germany*. Aldershot, England, and Burlington, VT: Ashgate, 2002.

Clements, Robert J., and Joseph Gibaldi. *Anatomy of the Novella: The European Tale Collection from Boccaccio and Chaucer to Cervantes*. New York: New York University Press, 1977.

Classen, Albrecht. "A Woman Fights for Her Honor: Ruprecht of Würzburg's *Von zwein koufmannen*: Female Self-Determination versus Male Mercantilism." *Seminar* 42 (2006): 95–113.

——. "'Die Heidin' — A Late-Medieval Experiment in Cultural Rapprochement Between Christians and Saracens." *Medieval Encounters* 11 (2005): 50–71.

——. "The Fourteenth-Century Verse Novella *Dis ist von dem Heselin*: Eroticism, Social Discourse, and Ethical Criticism." *Orbis Litterarum* 60 (2005): 260–77.

——. *Der Liebes- und Ehediskurs vom hohen Mittelalter bis zum frühen 17. Jahrhundert*. Volksliedstudien 5. Münster: New York, Waxmann, 2005.

——. "Love, Marriage, and Sexual Transgressions in Heinrich Kaufringer's Verse Narratives (ca. 1400)." In *Discourses on Love, Marriage, and Transgression in Medieval and Early Modern Literature*, ed. idem. Medieval and Renaissance Texts and Studies 278. Tempe, AZ: Arizona Center for Medieval and Renaissance Studies, 2005, 289-312.

——. "Gender Conflicts, Miscommunication, and Communicative Communities in the Late Middle Ages: The Evidence of Fifteenth-Century German Verse Narratives." In *Speaking in the Medieval World*, ed. Jean Godsall-Myers. Cultures, Beliefs and Traditions 16. Leiden: Brill, 2003, 65–92.

——. "Love and Marriage and the Battle of Genders in the Stricker's *maeren*." *Neuphilologische Mitteilungen* 92 (1991): 105–22.

Dunphy. *History as Literature: German World Chronicles of the Thirteenth Century in Verse. Excerpts from Rudolf von Ems Weltchronik, The Christherre-Chronik,*

Jans Enikel Weltchronik. Introduction, Translation, and Notes by R. Graeme Dunphy. Medieval German Texts in Bilingual Editions 3. Kalamazoo, MI: Medieval Institute Publications, 2003.

Fischer, Hanns. *Die deutsche Märendichtung des 15. Jahrhunderts*. Münchener Texte und Untersuchungen zur deutschen Literatur des Mittelalters 12. Munich: Beck, 1966.

———. *Studien zur deutschen Märendichtung*. Tübingen: Niemeyer, 1968. 2nd rev. and expanded ed. by Johannes Janota. Tübingen: Niemeyer, 1983.

Grubmüller, Klaus. *Die Ordnung, der Witz und das Chaos: Eine Geschichte der europäischen Novellistik im Mittelalter: Fabliau – Märe – Novelle*. Tübingen: Niemeyer, 2006.

———. *Kleinere Erzählformen im Mittelalter: Paderborner Colloquium 1987*, ed. Klaus Grubmüller, L. Peter Johnson, and Hans-Hugo Steinhoff. Schriften der Universität-Gesamthochschule-Paderborn, Reihe Sprach- und Literaturwissenschaft 10. Paderborn: Ferdinand Schöningh, 1988.

Haug, Walter, and Burghart Wachinger, eds. *Kleinere Erzählformen des 15. und 16. Jahrhunderts*. Fortuna vitrea 8. Tübingen: Niemeyer, 1993.

Jenny, Beat Rudolf. *Graf Froben Christoph von Zimmern: Geschichtsschreiber—Erzähler—Landesherr. Ein Beitrag zur Geschichte des Humanismus in Schwaben*. Lindau and Constance: J. Thorbecke, 1959.

Kocher, Ursula. *Boccaccio und die deutsche Novellistik: Formen der Transposition italienischer 'novelle' im 15. und 16. Jahrhundert*. Chloe: Beihefte zum Daphnis 38. Amsterdam and New York: Editions Rodopi, 2005.

Köpf, Gerhard. *Märendichtung*. Sammlung Metzler M 166. Stuttgart: Metzler, 1987.

Manutchehr-Danai, Mohsen. *Dictionary of Gems and Gemology*. Berlin: Springer-Verlag, 2000.

Meyer, Otto Richard. "Das Quellen-Verhältnis des 'Borten'." *Zeitschrift für deutsches Altertum und deutsche Literatur* 59 (1922): 36-46.

Mihm, Arend. *Überlieferung und Verbreitung der Märendichtung im Spätmittelalter*. Germanische Bibliothek, Dritte Reihe: Untersuchungen und Einzeldarstellungen. Heidelberg: Winter, 1967.

Millet, Victor. "Märe mit Moral? Zum Verhältnis von weltlichem Sinnangebot und geistlicher Moralisierung in drei mittelhochdeutschen Kurzerzählungen." In *Geistliches in weltlicher und Weltliches in geistlicher Literatur des Mittelalters*, ed. Christoph Huber, Burghart Wachinger, and Hans-Joachim Ziegeler. Tübingen: Niemeyer, 2000, 273–90.

Schirmer, Karl-Heinz. *Stil- und Motivuntersuchungen zur mittelhochdeutschen Versnovelle*. Hermaea: Germanistische Forschungen, Neue Folge 26. Tübingen: Niemeyer, 1969.

———, ed. *Das Märe: Die mittelhochdeutsche Versnovelle des späteren Mittelalters.* Wege der Forschung 558. Darmstadt: Wissenschaftliche Buchgesellschaft, 1983.

Schnell, Rüdiger, "Erzählstrategie, Intertextualität und 'Erfahrungswissen': Zu Sinn und Sinnlosigkeit spätmittelalterlicher Mären." In *Wolfram-Studien XVIII: Erzähltechnik und Erzählstrategien in der deutschen Literatur des Mittelalters: Saarbrücker Kolloquium 2002*, ed. Wolfgang Haubrichs, Eckart Conrad Lutz, and Klaus Ridder. Berlin: Erich Schmidt, 2004, 367–404.

Sprague, Maurice W. "Down the Rabbit-Hole: *Das Häslein*, Gottfried von Straßburg and Hartmann von Aue." *Jahrbuch der Oswald von Wolkenstein Gesellschaft* 15 (2005): 315–48.

Strasser, Ingrid. *Vornovellistisches Erzählen: Mittelhochdeutsche Mären bis zur Mitte des 14. Jahrhunderts und altfranzösische Fabliaux.* Philologica Germanica 10. Vienna: Fassbaender, 1989.

Wailes, Stephen L. "Courtly Diction in Middle High German 'maeren' in the Context of Latin and French Traditions." Ph.D. diss, Harvard University, 1968.

Zeyen, Stefan. *... daz tet der liebe dorn: Erotische Metaphorik in der deutschsprachigen Lyrik des 12.-14. Jahrhunderts.* Item mediävistische Studien 5. Essen: Item-Verlag, 1996.

Ziegeler, Hans-Joachim. *Erzählen im Spätmittelalter: Mären im Kontext von Minnereden, Bispeln und Romanen.* Münchener Texte und Untersuchungen zur deutschen Literatur des Mittelalters 87. Munich: Artemis Verlag, 1985.